Why Waiting
WORKS

HOW FAST SEX PREVENTS US FROM FINDING TRUE LOVE AND LONG-TERM HAPPINESS.

ROB B. KOWALSKI

ISBN 10: 1-68411-593-0
ISBN 13: 978-1-68411-593-8

Printed in the United States of America

"The road of excess
leads to the
palace of wisdom."

Walt Whitman

PRAISE FOR *WHY WAITING WORKS*
See what readers are saying...

I believe in this book

I believe what the author is saying. He doesn't pretend to know it all and he doesn't pretend to be perfect which is why I think I was drawn to it so much. It took me all of 36 hours to finish the book so if anyone has the opportunity the means and the time and you're reading this review I highly suggest to take those 36 hours to make a change to your entire life.
Alexus Neidert Real Estate Sales (Severna Park, MD)

The Greater The Sacrifice – The Greater The Reward

Why Waiting Works, addresses sex from a realistic, 2018 awareness, weighing both the male and female's challenges, needs, desires, and best interests. The author writes from the perspective of a man with both positive and negative real life experiences. Kowalski addresses the truth, makes you feel like you're in a conversation with a friend who's been there/done that, and coaches you through a plan for your future - all in one quick read. This book is not just for mid-life singles looking for love; it is for anyone who believes in the kind of love that is selfless, honoring, life-giving, protective, hopeful, patient, energizing, and won't fail! The sacrifice is fully worth the reward. My life is richer after having read this book.
Nicole Richert, Mortgage Banker (Houston, TX)

A thoughtful, well-written, and eye-opening book about pursuing relationships, and life, in a different way

A thoughtful, well-written, and eye-opening book about pursuing relationships, and life, in a different way. Rob has taken a concept that is so often feared in today's culture (waiting to have sex until marriage) and has broken it down into new and common sense ways that are easy to understand and hard to deny. He stresses delayed gratification instead of just having it all right now, and not just with love, but in every area of our lives.

Mike Nitti, Marketing & Communications (Baltimore, MD)

A must read! Wonderful book!

I would recommend *Why Waiting Works*. This book offers a great perspective on how to pursue healthy relationships, examine boundaries and build meaningful relationships. Kowalski takes the concept of waiting and explains how delayed gratification can have impact in all areas of one's life. Kowalski offers practical advice on how to approach this concept and how to break culture's rules to experience the best life that will result in a lifelong faithful relationships.

Daphne Chaniz-Rico RN, MSN (Newark, DE)

Must read for all women and men of all ages!!

Being introduced to this author via Youtube and sharing his principles around why waiting works has made a profound impact on my personal life. This is a must read for women and men of all ages and demographics who truly want to live a fulfilled life. Read this book and share it with anyone who is struggling to not only find love but to come to truly value themselves.

Joanne Crooks, Real Estate (Boston MA)

This book will change your life.

Rob's story is incredible, but he is just like you and me. We are all looking for fulfillment and we typically try to find it in the wrong places. *Why Waiting Works* is inspirational and practical. His story and the life lessons that he shares in this book will give you a new perspective and encourage you on your journey.

Jimmy Akers, Pastor (Fort Myers, FL)

Everyone needs to read this book

For anyone who has ever hit a dead end in any aspect of their life, you will be able to relate to this. The author takes you through the extremes of what hasn't worked for him and what has. *Why Waiting Works* is more than just a book about waiting to have sex before marriage, it's a about how patience, hard work, obedience, self love and appreciation can all lead to self-actualization and fulfillment. I wish I had read this in high school or college.

Izzie Arrizza, Clinical research Manager (Baltimore, MD)

Great advice and to the point

Great read. This book really spoke to me and opened my mind to things I've never thought about. We always talk to our GFs about why men act it do certain things and ask for their advice and this basically breaks it down in an open and honest way from a guys perspective. It totally makes sense. Def recommend reading it.

Romy Mittler, Makeup Artist (Boca Raton, FL)

Great perspective!

This is a great book for anyone who is interested in finding some clarity on how Men really think, what their view point is on dating, sex, and marriage. I would suggest getting some girlfriends together and discussing the chapters in this book!!

Melissa Bona, Entrepreneur (Annapolis, MD)

Why reading (*Why Waiting Works*) works!

I love this book! Inspiring & persuasive written in a very logical way, you could really relate to it! Personally it helped me to reevaluate my life in so many ways! I strongly recommend it for singles and parents of teens as well!

Magida Semaan, Insurance Broker (Beirut Lebanon)

Very insightful

I can relate and I agree with you. Thank God for your wisdom. The truth will set me free forever.

Anne Riddick (United Kingdom)

A NOTE TO YOU THE READER

No matter where you are on this journey, whether you are a virgin, you've been abstaining for years, you're just starting out, or you are currently sexually active not even sure about any of this, I know one thing for sure, we all have something in common; we want to get the most out of life. For you that might mean something different than others, it could mean reaching your full potential and making your greatest contribution, for others, it might just mean having the most fun and enjoying your time on this earth as much as possible. Whatever it means to you, I promise that if you commit to this journey of finding love before sex your life will be positively impacted in ways that right now you can't even imagine. Up front it's quite impossible to see, it's only when you begin the journey that you are fully able to comprehend all the benefits you receive from this one simple decision. That one good decision will lead to another and another and it becomes like dominoes until you look back and your whole life has changed. I refer to this as the compound effect.

If you are already on the journey of self-improvement it is like pouring rocket fuel onto whatever you are currently doing. You will become clearer about what you want to do and you will reach your goals faster than you could possibly imagine. The areas I've personally experienced SIGNIFICANT improvements are: my relationships, spirituality, self-esteem and my overall health.

As an author, speaker and Founder of a nonprofit my life's aim is to help as many people as possible see it's never too late to be who they might have been and give them the resources they need to make big changes quickly. I can say with absolute certainty that saving sex for love is the most practical decision you can make to realizing and achieving whatever it is you want MOST in life.

Thank you,
Rob Kowalski

A Special Invitation
The Why Waiting Works Community

Readers and followers of *Why Waiting Works* make up a stellar tribe of inspired individuals, applying (or ready to apply) the age-old concept of delayed gratification for finding true love and long-term happiness. Even though WWW is about sex, it's really about becoming the best version of yourself and the man or woman you were created to be.

The *Why Waiting Works Community* is about more than the book. It's a movement of like-minded individuals who want more and better for and from relationships. No one claims perfection in the movement but by all means necessary a desire to move in the right direction towards finding love before sex.

As the author of *Why Waiting Works,* I felt a sense of responsibility to create a space where others that are on this journey could connect with each other. I am honestly shocked at how engaged and thoughtful our members are. I had no idea it would become so popular and be a resource to so many like-minded people navigating their way through.

Visit bit.ly/WWWcommunity and request to join *The Why Waiting Community* on Facebook®. Here you'll be able to find inspiration, support, and encouragement as well as share information, discuss the book, post videos, and find an accountability partner.

I post and comment myself frequently and look forward to talking with you there.

If you enjoy this book, please leave a review. It will only take a few minutes and reviews help other readers discover this book.

To help me get this message out and earn rewards in the process become a member of my SUPERFAM! Go to WWW.ROBBKOWALSKI.COM and sign up today. You will be the first to get notified when I post new videos and promotions and I'll keep you updated on everything I'm working on.

As a thank you, subscribers get my 'Dating While Waiting Guide' absolutely Free.

I'd love to connect with you personally on social media, follow @RobBKowalski on Instagram, Facebook, YouTube and @RBKOWALSKI1 on Twitter. Please feel free to send me a direct message, leave a comment, or ask me a question. I do my best to answer every one, so let's connect!

CONTENTS

ACKNOWLEDGEMENTS

This project could not have been completed without the help of some very important people. First and foremost to the people that coached me along the way as I made this journey in order to learn these lessons, Chris and Lori Lockemy. Thank you both for always believing in me and for giving me grace when I needed it most. Thank you, Tangi Allen, for coming alongside me to help me get my thoughts on paper, and for being a good friend. Thank you, Staci Fields Cranor, for investing your time into this project, you are a true Godsend. Thank you to my mom Pam Swanegan Hart for being the amazing woman that you are and supporting all of my crazy dreams. Lastly, thank you to all my friends and fellow leaders in CityFam, I can't imagine how I would have ever made it without all of you; you add so much richness to my life.

PREFACE

It had been a long night of debauchery. The sun had already come up, and people filled our hotel room. Guys with their shirts off, jacked full of steroids and a bathtub full of naked girls. People walked in and out of the room to see the spectacle, some I barely knew. None of it fazed me. It was a pretty typical weekend for me. The only difference was, this time we were in Cancun, Mexico. A group of fifteen guys and girls had gone down for Spring Break. Even though most of us were in our mid-twenties, a little older than the average college student, we were immature for our age, so we figured it would work out.

It was my second consecutive year celebrating Spring Break in Cancun. The previous year we had spent a couple of nights at a club called Daddy-O's. If I'm honest, it was probably the most fun I'd ever had in my life. That year, a few of my buddies and I met up with some girls we knew from Baltimore. We were all rolling on ecstasy and dancing on tables. The girls were kissing each other when breasts started coming out. A crowd formed. The manager escorted us to a private VIP section overlooking the club.

The atmosphere was insane. Techno/hip-hop music blared, and hot, sweaty bodies gyrated in a hypnotic rhythm. It was pandemonium. The club owner sent over bottles of champagne, strawberries, and security guards ... free of charge. The nightclub was huge. The spotlight pointed directly at us, and the entire crowd of 1,000+ plus roared every time the girls flashed some skin. It was insane, even by my standards. The following year I brought my friends and some of their girlfriends back to experience Cancun nightlife for themselves. It was more of the same; the girls put on a show, and the crowd cheered. I'm sure the nightclub benefited from the circus being in town. But I couldn't shake the fact that it just wasn't the same as it had been the previous year. It just was not as much fun. I was trying to manufacture a feeling, and it didn't come close. Back in my hotel room, I partied with friends from all over the country. In the bathtub, were two smoking hot, buck naked girls, one of whom was my current girlfriend, yet somehow, I still felt numb, like something was missing. What could it be? I don't know that I stopped long enough to evaluate it thoroughly but looking back it was there. I mean I had everything I thought I wanted, everything the world told me would make me happy--money, women, and popularity. Yet, there was still a void, and I was chasing after something.

INTRODUCTION

Thank you for your willingness to pick up this book and give it a read. The fact that the title alone didn't scare you off is a testament to your open-mindedness. I decided to write a book on this taboo topic because I wanted to bring my unique perspective to the subject. They say, "ignorance is bliss," until it's not. Let me forewarn you. You may not agree with everything you read, and that's all right. There are some ideas contained in this book that will challenge you and everything you believe to be true about dating and sex.

Here's my charge to you: read this book all the way through. While there may be ideas you disagree with, I believe there's a lot contained in it that will help you. When you read something that stands out to you or that you disagree with, underline it or make notes on the side of the pages, and then join our discussion in the "Why Waiting Works Community" Facebook group. While my goal is not to argue with anyone about the topic, I do want to be honest about the problems I see with the way many people approach dating and sex today. I also want to share my own mistakes that have caused me, and others, pain. While others' experiences may not be as excessive as mine, these mistakes are still widespread, and I believe you will be able to relate.

* * * * * *

Throughout this book, we will take a closer look at how the subject of sex touches every area of our lives; and how the one decision to wait for sex can affect your entire future, and ultimately determine if you reach your full potential in life. Even though this book is about sex, it is also about becoming the best version of yourself, and the man or woman you were created to be. Again, my only hope is to shed some light on a very misunderstood, but vital to understand, subject so that you can have everything you want most in life.

"Why Waiting Works" is part autobiography, part roadmap, for finding the love of your life and the life you've always wanted. The lessons I have learned in life, and in love (or lack thereof), were discovered the hard way. Even though I view the subject of sex through a Christian lens, the principles are universal. I believe you will gain a fresh view on how to find real love that, to many, may seem antiquated.

My book is different because most people who tell you it's a good idea to wait to have sex probably did not have sex before marriage. The reasons they might give would sound something like, *"it's a sin," "you're breaking a commandment,"* or else they would warn you about STD's or getting pregnant. While you may or may not believe those things to be true, or even if you do, they still may not make a lot of sense.

I remember going to church as a kid, and those principles not making sense to me. I was not about to buy into any of that *"the Bible says so"* nonsense. Well, I am here to state up front, that I have had a lot of sex outside of marriage, with a hell of a lot more people than the average man or woman. I've also been abstinent for years. I've lived at complete polar ends of the spectrum, maybe more so than any human being. In this book, I will provide practical reasons why waiting to have sex until marriage makes sense for everyone, regardless of faith affiliation or lack thereof.

CHAPTER ONE
ABOUT ME

"Sometimes the people with the worst past,
create the best future."
Umar bin al Khattab

I think it is important for my readers to know my background, so you understand my perspective. I'm no altar boy, far from it. I have not always believed the things I do now. At the risk of making myself look like a complete douchebag, I will share stories with you about my past to solidify points, hoping you can draw parallels from my experience and relate them to your own. So, let's get into it.

Since I was a boy, I've been fascinated by women. Maybe it comes from being raised by a single mom; I'm not sure. But success with women was a high priority for me. From the time I hit puberty, I guess you could say I was "girl crazy." I found the female species mysterious and fascinating. Many of my decisions, mostly the bad ones, were all based on whether it would help or hurt me "get girls." So, it seems natural to me now to write a book about sex because it was such a focus of mine for so much of my life that I've come to learn many things on the subject along the way. Plus, there is so much bad advice out there that it's time someone gave it to you straight.

* * * * * *

My mother became pregnant with me at the tender age of fourteen. She and my dad got married before I was born. Surprise, it didn't last long. Growing up with a young mother and no father in the picture, I raised myself in many ways. I taught myself how to be a man. No one ever talked to me about sex or modeled what it meant to be a man, so I just kind of figured it out as I went along.

I'd like to think if I'd had a father figure in my life that I would have learned to respect and value women more. I'm not sure how I would have turned out if my dad were in the picture, but he wasn't. I accept responsibility for all my actions, but I wonder what life would have been like if my dad had been around more to model what a loving relationship looked like with my mother. Many times, we think our actions only hurt us, and we don't realize we affect future generations.

A boy needs a male role model to look up to, to teach him the ways of the world. Whether it be a father or a father figure, boys need a strong example of what it means to be a man. Learning it from television and movies provides a tainted view of the world and manhood. My mother is a great woman. She did an amazing job raising me with only an eighth grade education and no financial support from my father. But a single mom alone can't teach a boy how to be a man. Single mothers should be commended and celebrated for trying to fill both roles in the absence of a father. However, a boy needs someone to play sports with, wrestle around with, teach them how to shave, tie a tie, talk to about deep things and even bust their butt when they mess up. I saw friends who had fathers, and I wanted that kind of relationship too. They went camping, and their fathers took them to the BMX track, and just spent time with them. I gravitated toward these kids; subconsciously longing for that kind of relationship with my own dad, but it wasn't to be. I had a couple of uncles, one a good role model and the other not so good. But they weren't in my life enough to fulfill my needs.

My uncle Gordy was and still is a good man. He did his best to help my mom while working two full-time jobs. He even put me in Christian schools for a couple of years, which I was quickly expelled from due to my rebellious nature. To this day, my Uncle Gordy is the father I never had. My stepfather John is a good man as well. He began dating my mom when I was fourteen, and he did a good job of keeping me out of the trouble I'm sure I would have gotten into had he not been around.

Because of my lack of a consistent male role model, and to be honest, my self-centered curiosity, my selfish approach to sex started at an early age. My friends and I talked incessantly about how we could not wait to lose our virginity and sleep with girls, even my buddies from church. When I was fifteen years old, I found a videotape on the coffee table my mom and her friends had rented of male exotic dancers. I put it in the VCR, watched a little of it, and decided right then and there that I wanted to be an exotic dancer. I used to say to my friends "what better job can there be than to have women stick money in your pants?" It's comical to me now, but it's true. While some kids dream of being cops, engineers, and bankers, I aspired to be a male stripper.

When I was nineteen years old, my four-year dream of becoming a male stripper came true. Over the next several years I worked my way up the ranks and went on to become the top guy for every entertainment agency in my hometown of Baltimore. That just meant when someone called the agency, I got first dibs on the show. I was doing upward of fifteen to twenty private shows a week. These were mostly birthday and bachelorette parties at women's houses. I joined a Male Revue and traveled to different clubs doing shows in the tri-state area. I guess you could say I was the original Magic Mike. My stripper friends and I (guys and girls) would all meet up after our performances and hit the nightclubs together. One night, a club owner approached me and asked me to promote a night at his club. The concept was simple, throw a party on a night the club was dead, and we could keep half of the cover charges at the door. It was a bad deal in hindsight. But, it sounded fun and would help me get girls. So, I eagerly accepted and began throwing parties in nightclubs.

A NEW BEGINNING

At the age of twenty-seven, I was running the nightlife in Baltimore and beginning to take over Washington DC. I had weekly parties at clubs in both cities that were the most popular nights of their week. I was still stripping on the weekend but planning an exit so that I could promote full time. My life was a party, and I was getting paid well to live it. I loved being me. Lots of late, drug-induced nights were par for the course. Along the way, I had more than my share of casual sex and failed relationships too.

Then one day in March of 2000 on a trip to Cancun, Mexico for Spring Break I heard God's voice for the very first time. I had a life-changing encounter with Jesus Christ, and everything began to change. Record skip! Say what?! Yes, that's right, for the first time in my life, I heard God's voice. It wasn't audible, but it was unmistakable. God told me He had a plan for my life and asked me to trust Him and to follow Him.

I accepted Jesus as my savior, which just involved me agreeing to follow Him, and that is when my life began to change.

Up until that point, if you had asked me if I were a Christian, I would have said yes (Christian was even my stripper name, but that's another story). *I mean I live in America, and my grandmom is a Christian, so of course, I am too.* That would have been my thought process in response to that question. Plus, I would have been too afraid to say, "no I'm not a Christian," because then what was I? An atheist? However, when I saw people praying, I, wasn't sure anyone was listening.

Gratification and excess consumed my life. Everything I did revolved around whether it would bring me more pleasure. Even my workouts weren't for health reasons. I went to the gym, so I could pick up more girls. I did what felt good when it felt good, and that was that. So, when God called me, I distinctly remember thinking, "What in the hell does God want with me? I am the LEAST religious person I know!" It's important to me that I not come off as self-righteous to anyone who reads this book. But, I'd be remiss if I didn't include this part of my story because finding God (or Him finding me) was the turning point in my life. It is the ONLY REASON I stopped living the way I had been living and learned the things about sex and dating that I'm about to share.

Jesus is the Lord of my life. He rescued me, and I don't know where I would be without Him. However, I still don't view myself as religious. I go to bars (even though I've been sober several years). I cuss more than I should. I love a good party, etc. But if you read the Bible, Jesus wasn't religious either. He hung out with sinners and prostitutes, NOT religious people. If you read the Bible, you'll learn that it was the religious people who killed Jesus because he flipped everything upside down.

THE BEST APOLOGY IS CHANGED BEHAVIOUR

After my encounter with Jesus, everything began to change in my life. I made the most radical 180-degree turn a person could. I went from being the most promiscuous guy I knew to being abstinent for the next six years. Yeah, let that sink in for a moment ... SIX YEARS! That includes every single day, every single night, weekends, holidays, leap years, all that. To say I was determined to wait would be a gross understatement.

Initially, the idea of waiting was stupid; sex, to me, was like a massage, *if it feels good do it!* I used to say and lived my life as such. But my days of excess taught me many lessons about what does and doesn't work, and why. I gave away all my costumes and never stripped another day in my life. I called up the entertainment agencies I worked for and had them cancel all my shows. I also quit promoting immediately, knowing the lifestyle wasn't conducive to this new one I was about to pursue. I couldn't be the party boy everyone had come to know anymore, influencing people to make decisions I was starting to see as dangerous. I was twenty-seven years old and didn't know what I would do to earn money, but I had a taste of God's power and trusted Him enough to believe He wouldn't let me starve. Another thing I did was break up with my beautiful, young girlfriend. I knew enough to know if I wanted to sleep with other girls, and not just her, I wasn't in love. I wasn't sure what God had for me, but I was ready to follow Him with all that was in me.

The first eighteen months were rough to say the least. God didn't tell me what to do next. I had this amazingly powerful conversion experience, and heard God call me so clearly asking me to follow Him, and then nothing. Not a peep for a year and a half.

I had a little over $20,000 saved from stripping and playing the stock market when I began to follow Him, but after a year and a half of not working, that was all gone, and my credit cards were maxed. During that period, I went from being popular party boy to home-bound Bible geek. I spent most of my time alone because I cut off all of my old friends, so that I wouldn't fall back into my old lifestyle. I knew hanging out with them would have spelled bad news for me. As determined as I was to do the right thing, I was still very weak from years of giving my flesh whatever it wanted. I kept my distance from them and went to church on Sundays, but not much else. Plus, my friends couldn't relate to me anymore, and I couldn't pretend like what happened wasn't real. After a year and a half, I ended up getting a job at a local gym, and while it wasn't my dream job, it paid the bills.

I was pursuing God as hard as I knew how. I read the Bible cover to cover a couple of times and was learning as much as I could about it all. I abstained from sex believing God would send me Mrs. Right to reward me for my good behavior at some point, and I would get married. I had had a lot of sex in my life, but at twenty-seven years of age I had never been in love, and I wanted to experience that. I also wanted to have guilt-free sex. I believed with some dedication to His ways, God would surely reward me. Plus, I felt like He had told me He had someone picked out for me if I waited, so I did. At first, the concept of waiting to have sex made no sense. To me, it was just two people giving each other what they wanted. But out of my desire to be obedient, I waited even if I didn't understand it completely.

It was a very lonely time for me and extremely difficult, but I was also very determined. It was an essential time in hindsight because I learned how to be okay with being single. My entire adult life I had either had a girlfriend or some girl I was dating and sleeping with. Learning to manage that appetite proved very beneficial for me and started to teach me how bad rebounding and dating out of loneliness can be. But I missed having friends and a social life, so I began looking for a group of people I could hang out with on the weekends. I wondered, what do people who are attempting to live this way do for fun? I liked the people I met at church, they were very nice, but a lot of them also seemed a little weird to me. I didn't relate to most of them very well, and they weren't doing much of anything I considered fun on the weekends. The people I did relate to the most were in the bars and clubs.

Every few months or so I would meet up with some old friends at a club out of sheer boredom, but often when I did, I'd end up drinking too much or doing something I regretted, so this became less and less of a viable option for me. Then a few months would go by, and I'd get so pent up with my lack of social interaction I'd go back out and try it again. Most weekends I wound up just going to the movies by myself or with a buddy, trying to avoid trouble. Over time I became very disillusioned. "Is this what my life will be like now?" "Will I ever enjoy life again?" I wondered. It was the hardest time of my life, and it lasted for six long years. God gave me the assurance He would send my soulmate to me, and we would live happily ever after, I figured that would fix the loneliness problems I was having.

Had God not given me the assurance He would send my soulmate to me, I'm sure I would have done what most people do when they get to the point of loneliness and depression I did. I would have starting dating and probably sleeping around again. Then I would never have realized the magnitude of the problem I'm about to share with you, nor would I have written this book.

After the better part of a decade of trying to be a good Christian boy, I got burnt out. I wanted to enjoy life with people I could relate to again, so I started going to the only places I knew to socialize and find other people like me--the bars. I was thirty-three years old and ready to have a social life again and be around some girls. I had abstained from having sex for several years, so I felt strong enough to handle the new freedom I began to give myself. I craved relationships and was ready to meet people and have some fun.

I hadn't had sex in six years (my first six-year stretch) and felt pretty good about who I was and felt like God was pleased with me. That summer I started feeling restless at the gym I managed. At the suggestion of some friends, I began praying about getting back into promoting again and felt like God was sending me signs to do it. I was shocked! I never thought I'd promote again. But I felt I was getting the green light, and I started to see how I could help people who were hurting if I were close to the edge. I had missed promoting desperately. It was the one thing that I felt like I was a natural at. But I still couldn't believe God was leading me back to that world. With no real plan and a mortgage that needed to be paid I left my job at the gym and started promoting again.

At this point no one knew who I was anymore. Some friends told me it was a bad decision, but I didn't listen. I felt like I could make a difference from the inside. It didn't take long for me to take over the nightlife. Three months after forming my company I had the hottest club in the city on Saturday nights, Kasbah. We were packing it out at 800 people, and it was the place to go, everyone was talking about it. On Thursdays I lead a Bible study in the club and we would go out afterward and feed the homeless. We were reading Rick Warren's "The Purpose Driven Life." On Saturdays I would tell my doormen, that if anyone came from the small group let them bypass the line and the $10 cover, and let them in for free. I wanted to reward people for making better decisions.

The Thursday night Bible study took off, it went from eight people attending every week to over forty. We had coke heads and strippers coming, it was a dream come true! These were MY people, and it was amazing … for a little while. We fixed up a shelter for homeless and battered women and dropped off gifts at Christmas to needy families. It was awesome. I quickly became popular again, and girls wanted to get to know me. But, I started to realize I was weaker than I thought and tried to keep my distance as much as possible; staying in on the nights we didn't have an event. I had moved into the city a short time earlier and was church shopping. I didn't have a lot of accountability and was still drinking on the nights I worked. Then one night after being out at a bar with friends I slept with a girl. I think I was more disappointed that I had broken my six-year streak than I was that I had disobeyed God. As bad as it sounds, saying that I hadn't had sex in all those years was a badge of honor for me. Now that I didn't have it I feared I wouldn't be able to maintain any level of obedience in this area. I was right. It wasn't long that I slept with a second girl, and then a third. I kept it quiet because I was leading a bible study and knew how bad it looked. Some people in the group found out about it and judged me pretty harshly, and rightfully so. It was painful.

I stepped down from leading the group and turned it over to a young pastor at a church I had recently started attending called Epic. The guy's name is Chris Lockemy, and he was young, relevant, hip, and a good replacement for me. I still attended the group and did my best to bring in others. I didn't want to lead it until I could get my act together, which I was sure I could do if I tried harder. Even with those mess ups I had cultivated a great group of friends and was enjoying life more than ever as a follower of Christ. We volunteered together, had dinner parties at each other's houses, and many of us attended church together on Sundays; it was a magical time for me. But stepping down from leadership, while it seemed to be the right move at the time, proved to be the worst thing I could have done. I was a successful, popular, nightclub promoter making money with almost no accountability and girls after me. The years I had sheltered myself produced all this pent-up energy that came raging back. I had a desire to be obedient to God, but I couldn't do it most of the time.

I started making more mistakes, usually with women. I hated how I felt the next day; a plethora of emotions, mostly emptiness, guilt, and depression would come flooding in. I attempted to quit drinking on several occasions, once I even went six weeks, which is an eternity when you are a nightclub promoter. I knew drinking wasn't technically a sin, but it led me to sin just about every time I did it because all my "mistakes" were on nights when I drank. The first date I went on in seven years was with a beautiful hometown hottie who had been coming to my events. I had seen her around and thought she looked like trouble, but our paths kept crossing, and she made my blood boil whenever I saw her, so I asked her out. Plus, I figured I could be a good example to her and lead her to Jesus. (Side note: never missionary date, it's a bad idea.) We ended up sleeping together pretty quickly and started dating. I knew she wasn't "the one" but I hoped having a steady girl around I would not mess up with others, which I was starting to do more regularly. Over the next few years as my promotion career took off my life as a whole spiraled downward, and for the most part, I became the person I was before ever meeting God. Except now it was worse because I felt guilty and like a complete failure.

Fast forward a few years. In 2011 I was at an all-time low. I was in a dead-end relationship; I hated what I did for a living, owed money in taxes, was losing my house to foreclosure, had a drug and alcohol problem, and had a pending DUI charge I had to face. On top of all that my dad got diagnosed with stage-four prostate cancer; talk about rock bottom. How did I get here I thought? My intentions were so good. I decided right then and there to rededicate myself to Christ. I was desperate and willing to do whatever it took to improve my life. There was a part of me that felt hopeless too, though. I felt like I had already tried this before and given it everything I had, and I still couldn't do it. *Why would this time be different?* I wondered. I met with Pastor Chris and told him I was ready to come home. He challenged me and said, "okay then it starts today." I knew he meant radical change. God says He'd rather us be cold than lukewarm. He says it makes Him want to spit us out of his mouth.

Think about it – when something should be hot, coffee for instance, has sat around and gotten tepid, it does make you want to spit it out. What God is saying is He'd rather us be against Him and be real about it than say we're a follower of Jesus but live like the world. At least when you are ice cold, like I was at the time, you have a pretty good chance of hitting bottom and coming to Him in your crisis. When you're lukewarm you just kind of drift along not doing too bad but not accomplishing the purpose He has for you either. As unnatural as the cleaner lifestyle had felt to me in many ways, living life the way I had been was killing me, and I needed to make a change. If when I initially gave my life to God, I did a 180, I guess you could say I did a 540. But, I knew there were people in those bars I'd hung out in for so long who were like me and needed to know there was another way. Rather than commit to leaving the bar scene altogether, I decided to get myself together and one day go back and take my new life to that scene and to the people there who so desperately need it.

I'll get to the rest of this story later ...

* * * * * *

Once I cleared out the gutter, I redirected my sexual energy into working on myself. It was difficult. Initially, I thought of my former way of life and sex constantly. I started working on the big things at first, like sex and alcohol, which, honestly caused me to want to have sex and use drugs to numb my pain and discomfort. But, as I denied myself these things, the intensity of my sexual appetite slowly started to decrease. The time I spent going to bars and chasing women was replaced by involving myself in church. I began volunteering heavily through a local church, doing various projects and helped as many people around me as often as I could. In some ways, helping others became my new addiction. Except the results were all positive. As I started to see the fruit of making better decisions, it fueled me to do even more. I began reading personal development books and sought to remove other negative influences from my life that were holding me back. Ironically, in directing my energy outward in an attempt to better the lives of others around me, I created a better, more satisfying life for myself. I'm still a work in progress. While I may not be where I want to be, thank God I'm not where I used to be.

CHAPTER TWO
EVERYBODY ELSE IS DOING IT

"Observe the masses and do the opposite"
James Caan

There are many reasons, which we will get into later, why waiting to have sex until marriage works. But first, I've heard it said that the best advice is to "observe the masses and do the opposite." It's not hard to see how this philosophy would be a good one to subscribe to, especially when it comes to dating and sex. One of the most persuasive arguments that waiting might be the right tactic is, in fact, that everybody else is doing it, and I don't mean that everyone else is waiting either. I mean everyone is *doing it* and doing it quickly.

Let's be honest; numbers don't lie. Polls reveal that the average number of dates a couple in the United States goes on these days before sleeping together is three. Apparently, the "three-date rule" is still alive and well in this country. In case you didn't know, the rate of divorce in the United States is fifty percent. So, what does all this mean to you? It means your chances of getting married and being happy are very low if you go about this like everyone else does. The definition of insanity is continuing to do the same thing, expecting a different result. With all this evidence and personal experience, why do we expect to do what everyone else is doing and get a different outcome? Probably because of the fun of the moment; sex feels great! On top of that, most of us don't like discipline, and we dislike waiting for things we want even less.

But, do more sexual partners equal greater happiness? Research suggests the answer to that question is no. In reality, the most sexually satisfied among us have one partner. Yep, one. Now, we know sex makes us happy, and the more sex we have, the happier we are, but it's the frequency with which we have it, not the number of partners we have.

We have all heard the saying that variety is the spice of life, so wouldn't it make sense that a variety of partners would spice up one of the most enjoyable experiences we get as humans? It turns out, the opposite is true. People with more sexual partners are not as happy as those who are monogamous. Spouses who cheat are less happy than faithful partners. Men who go to prostitutes are typically the unhappiest, not only with their wives but with themselves as well.

Studies have also reported that the more sexual partners one has before marriage, the unhappier that person will be in his or her marriage. Research conducted by University of Denver professors for The National Marriage Project dealt with this topic. Their year-long study included 1,000 couples ages eighteen to thirty-four; 418 of the couples got married during the study. Twenty-three percent of the participants abstained from having sex with anyone other than their spouse. That twenty-three percent reported enjoying marriage the most. One potential takeaway from this study is that people who have more partners before getting married become more easily dissatisfied with their married sex life and their spouse. The research has its detractors, but my own experience falls right in line with this study. Sleeping around did not make me happier, and the people I knew then who slept with multiple partners did not go on to have happy marriages.

My heart goes out to those who've experienced divorce. No one marries thinking they won't make it. However, divorce rates are skyrocketing in this country. There are a lot of good people I know who are divorced.

To them, I say, if you know you did the best you could for your marriage and your spouse, lift up your head. There is no shame nor judgment. Be encouraged. I believe that even in that experience there is a lesson and a higher purpose for you.

* * * * * *

Could it be that our desire to have sex too quickly is leading us to date and even marry the wrong people? I believe the answer is yes. Let's look at this practically, because I'm not here merely to tell you to stop having sex. But, instead, to offer some objective advice about why having sex before you get to know the other person could be the cause of many of your woes.

Why is this the case? Because there's more to a relationship than sex. When you don't pump the brakes, you can easily wind up in something complicated with someone you do not know very well because SEX CONNECTS US. That's what it was designed to do.

Like Morpheus said to Neo in one of my favorite movies of all time, The Matrix, "This is your last chance. After this, there is no turning back." If you are afraid to learn something new that will help you change the way you think, and ultimately live, this is the time to close the book. Remember, all I'm offering is the truth, nothing more.

CHAPTER THREE
SEX CONNECTS US

"Although we've come to the end of the road
Still I can't let you go It's unnatural, you belong to me,
I belong to you"
Boyz II Men – End Of The Road Lyrics

I'm glad you had the courage to keep reading. While you may not be convinced that waiting works yet, I believe the average amount of time people are waiting to have sex, and the skyrocketing divorce rate proves to us, undeniably, that *not* waiting isn't working. One of the biggest reasons it doesn't work is because, as I teased in the previous chapter, SEX CONNECTS US. That is what it was designed to do.

My first real girlfriend, we will call her "Lisa," was when I twenty years old, and my career as a male stripper was beginning to take off. One day after a revue a few of the guys I stripped with and I went to a local bar named River Watch in Baltimore. I met Lisa for the first time. She told me she was married, but on the outs with her husband. Lisa had large breast implants, drove a nice sports car, and wore G-string underwear. I was a real dirt-bag at the time, so I knew all I needed to know to get her number and ask her out on a date. To me, Lisa was a step up. She was slightly older than me and hotter than the girls I was used to dating. My friends seemed impressed that a twenty-year-old punk from Brooklyn, Maryland could score a woman like Lisa.

We had sex on the first date. I wasn't looking for anything at this point in my life except fun. I assumed she felt the same way. With my career as a male stripper beginning to take off and with it the opportunity to date more women, the last thing I wanted was to be tied down in a relationship. I made that clear up front to any girl I hung out with, including Lisa.

Over that summer we continued dating and sleeping together. I tried to limit how many times I saw Lisa during the week, so I could still enjoy a certain level of freedom. I consistently reminded Lisa that I wasn't looking for anything too serious. I was sleeping with other girls on the side, which I reasoned was okay because I was honest with Lisa that we weren't in a committed relationship. I wasn't necessarily sharing details about what I was doing when we weren't together, but technically I wasn't lying either. Even though I had made this decision to limit how often I saw her, we inadvertently started spending more time with each other. Sure enough, a weeknight would come around that I didn't have plans. Lisa would call and offer to bring dinner over and rent a movie from Blockbuster (it was still open at this time), how could I refuse? She would spend the night at my house, and we would have sex.

Lisa stayed, and as the weeks went by, I began to develop stronger feelings for her. There was a part of me that knew I wasn't in love and still wanted to be free to date other women. The other part of me loved the idea of being with Lisa. Even though she was not asking to be my girlfriend, I knew she wanted to be, and it was starting to cause fights between us. I felt obligated to make her my girlfriend because she had stuck around, so I owed her.

On top of that, I was starting to feel territorial over her, like she was mine. I didn't want her to date or sleep with anyone else. When you're having regular sex with someone, there is an unspoken expectation that the other person is not sleeping around. I knew I couldn't play the non-committal game for much longer and would need to make her my girlfriend or stop seeing her altogether.

One night, during sex, I asked Lisa to be my girlfriend. She said yes. Within two months we rented an apartment and moved in together. It was not long before I knew something was missing in our relationship. I had strong urges for other women, but not so much for the beautiful girl lying next to me every night. It got to the point that, on most nights, I preferred sleep to sex with her. When we did have sex, it felt like I was merely fulfilling my duty as a boyfriend.

With my career as a stripper on a steady incline, I was doing more shows than ever. However, my new girlfriend hated my profession. Since I was stripping when she met me, Lisa could not say much. Although, I'm sure she thought she could change me. As these feelings of restlessness continued to grow over time, I began to cheat. Lisa suspected, but could never prove it. I would have recurring thoughts, wondering if I could be happier with other women. I subconsciously began keeping a mental Rolodex of girls I planned to date (a.k.a. have sex with) when we "broke up." I tried to write all this off as normal, figuring most men in relationships felt the same way. I assumed my feelings would come around sooner or later, and I would "learn to love her." You hear it all the time, "relationships take work," maybe this is what they mean.

While I was not happy at home, I could not bring myself to break up with Lisa either. She was very emotionally invested in me, so I thought it would crush her to let her go. In some ways, I told myself I was doing her a favor by staying. When in reality, I was a coward.

Our relationship lasted for four years. Finally, one day, I worked up the courage to tell her I wasn't sure if I was in love with her. It was the hardest thing I had ever done up to that point in my life. We both cried a lot and not long after, I moved out. I was sad but also relieved on some level. I felt like I could breathe again.

Soon after we split, Lisa met another guy at her gym and started dating him. Unexpectedly, it drove me crazy. The girl I had spent four years with was now seeing someone else. It felt like a security blanket had been ripped away, and I needed it back.

Suddenly, it was like I had no control over my emotions, and I felt torn in two directions. I began pursuing Lisa, trying to convince her to come back while exercising my newfound freedom as a single man, going out to the bars and clubs. In some ways, I felt like a caged animal that had been set free.

I was twenty-four years old and doing more shows than any male stripper in Baltimore. I was in the phone book, so I thought I had arrived. On any given Friday or Saturday, I had parties lined up every hour from 2:00 pm to 12:00 midnight. I took advantage of being single, openly dating and hooking up with different girls. All the while, I was trying to convince my ex-girlfriend to come back to me. I don't know what I was thinking. All I knew was that when I saw Lisa, I missed her. It hurt ... and it hurt a lot.

The thought of Lisa dating and sleeping with another guy killed me. I had never experienced pain like that in my life, and I had a hard time dealing with it. Then, one morning after several months of being apart she called and asked if I wanted her to come over. I said yes. She did. We had sex four times that day. There's no sex like makeup sex. It was hot and passionate because I still had feelings for the girl.

I remember how grateful I felt when she came back. *This time it will be different.* It was amazing ... for about a week. I remember the feeling of restlessness creeping back in and thinking to myself, *You idiot! What did you do? You were free!* The problem is I had created a soul tie with Lisa. I didn't know what it meant, and it would be years before I heard that term, but I know that is what I was feeling with Lisa.

For those unfamiliar with the term "soul ties," it's a "Christianese" term. In its simplest form, a soul tie is an intense bond with another person formed during intercourse. Soul ties draw people together that may have otherwise hated and run from each other. If you've ever seen a beaten and abused woman return to a man that treats her like dirt, you have witnessed a soul tie's power. A soul tie is a bond that helps a married couple survive the storms of life. Or it can be a negative connection keeping two people that shouldn't be together, and for a long time, if not indefinitely.

It's hard to say how long it takes for a soul tie to form. I believe it's different for everyone and can be different for each person you choose to sleep with. I'd venture to say; it's possible to form a soul tie after having sex one time. Therefore, people, often women, become clingy after sex. But one thing is certain, the more times you have sex, the stronger the soul tie becomes. How many times have you seen that couple that breaks up and keeps getting back together? They cannot overcome the soul connection they made through sex. Even though they may not love the other person, they may, in fact, hate them, but that soul tie is stronger than their will to break free from it.

There I was, back in a relationship with a girl I had spent the past four years with, hoping it would be different. Yet, wondering how I would escape if it weren't. We opted not to move back in together. I stayed in the place I had rented as an insurance policy, in case things didn't work out. The dynamics returned rather quickly to the way they were when we lived together previously. Lisa and I stuck it out for another year until we finally broke up again.

This time, Lisa started dating a male fitness model on the West Coast and once again, it threw me for a loop. I was crazy jealous and tried to get her back. The depression was almost unbearable. I knew I was caught up in something beyond my control. Helpless to resist, I wanted the pain to stop.

I went all in, telling her I would quit stripping, move back in with her, and that we could get engaged if she came back. Fortunately for me, this time Lisa did not come back. She married the male model and moved to California. I didn't have to see her around town with him or anyone else. It worked out well for me in the end. But, what a whirlwind of emotions. On the other side of it, I was like *what was that!* I had no control over myself.

· · · · · ·

Howard Stern once said, "People get married for one of two reasons: they're in love, or about to break up." In my case, that was spot on. All you need is to look at the biology behind sex to see why this statement is true. During sex, there is a hormone released called oxytocin. Women are hard-wired to be trusting and to become deeply attached when this happens. Oxytocin is referred to as the love, cuddle, or bonding hormone. "It increases the feelings of love, well-being, peace, affection, nurturing, security, and attachment and causes humans to want to stay together and organize as family units. It's the glue of the family structure," writes Sandra Brown in her book "Women Who Love Psychopaths."

This "glue" bonds couples together, making a woman feel attached to a man after sex, and over time, causing a man to feel territorial over a woman. The more times people have sex, the stronger the bond. That bond makes breaking up hard. Oxytocin is the reason intimate relationships are so much more painful to end than non-sexual relationships. Oxytocin can also make people stay in relationships longer than they should. Many Scientists believe this chemical is the key to sustaining a monogamous relationship.

Sex is essentially the connection mechanism that's been hard-wired into us. While sex cannot make you fall in love with someone, if you have it too early with the wrong person, it can damn sure mimic "feelings of love." Sex can make you feel like you are in love with the person when all you have in common with them is lust. When this bond takes place during sex, relationships become more complicated. Sex changes the dynamics of relationships. Bringing sex into a relationship too quickly distorts your ability to evaluate whether the person would have simply been a good friend or a potential mate for life.

●　●　●　●　●　●

One of the most significant problems with having sex early in a relationship is creating a bond with a virtual stranger. If the average number of dates a couple goes on in this country before sleeping together is three, this is a problem because they are sleeping with ... creating soul ties with ... someone they don't know well. It takes longer than that to find out who that person really is. I mean, how well can you possibly know someone after a few dates? A person could pretend to be anyone during that time. They could be completely crazy! Still, the average couple will have sex before they truly know each other. Many of us do the same thing hoping our situation will be different, even though we know the odds of success in following that path are slim. "It's said that a wise person learns from their mistakes. A wiser one learns from the mistakes of others." (John Maxwell).

CHAPTER FOUR
TO CLEAVE OR NOT TO CLEAVE?

"Therefore, shall a man leave his father and his mother, and shall cleave unto his wife: and they shall be one flesh."
Genesis 2:24

The first mention of monogamy in the Bible is in Genesis. The Bible says, "a man (shall) leave his father and his mother, and shall cleave unto his wife: and they shall be one flesh." Some translations say, "the two are united into one," (a.k.a. soul tie). The word cleave is defined as "stick or hold together and resist separation, to join fast together, to glue, cement." This sounds a lot like Oxytocin doesn't it? I now believe that God designed sex to help us stick together so we become one and can make it through all the ups and downs of life once we find our person to preserve the family unit. The problem with treating sex like it's recreation is you can't become one with more than one. The more people we sleep with, the more of ourselves we give away; the more of someone else's spirit we carry with us.

Imagine if when you had sex with a person, you became physically joined at the hip. Wherever they go, you go. Wherever you go, they go. This joining happens emotionally and spiritually when we have sex; we attach our soul to another, and yet we have no idea where they are going. We can easily cleave to the wrong person before ever getting to know who they truly are. Then we wonder why we are unhappy but can't seem to break up. Then when we do break up, we wonder why it hurts so deeply and leaves us feeling scarred. This is the obvious reason sex was never meant to be outside of marriage because it hurts to split that apart. If you go back to my imaginary scenario above, you get the image of two people being violently cut apart. Sex was always supposed to come after we meet someone we connect with on a deep level, after getting to know them **outside** of the bedroom. Then and only then were we supposed to get physical, thus sealing our commitment to them and "cleaving together."

* * * * * *

Many studies have been done on the benefits of waiting to have sex, and the research is clear. The longer one delays the onset of sexual activity in a relationship, the more favorable the relationship outcome. Here are some compelling stats: A 2012 study by Cornell University surveyed couples about their relationship happiness, habits, and other intimate questions. Researchers said that participants who waited at least six months to have sex with their partners were happier than those who didn't. They enjoyed, "higher relationship stability, higher relationship satisfaction, better communication, and higher quality sexual relationship."

Another study in the American Psychological Association's Journal of Family Psychology revealed that couples who wait until they are married to have sex appear to be much happier than those who race to get it on. The study was based on 2,035 married individuals who participated in an online assessment, which included questions such as, "When did you become sexual in this relationship?" A statistical analysis of participants showed that couples who wait until they put a ring on it enjoy significantly more benefits than those who had sex earlier: "Relationship satisfaction was rated twenty percent higher and sexual quality of the relationship was rated fifteen percent better among those couples that waited until marriage to have sex." I don't know about you but that sounds like good news to me.

What's even better, is that the study was "controlled for religion," meaning even for people who considered themselves non-religious, waiting to have sex produced the same benefits regardless of faith affiliation (or lack thereof). Couple this with the extremely low divorce rate among couples that waited until marriage to have sex alongside the higher divorce rate for people with the highest number of sexual partners and the picture starts to become very clear.

These studies clearly prove that waiting works, and not waiting costs us down the road. Lead study author Dean Busby, a professor at Brigham Young University's School of Family Life, said in a release that couples who waited at least thirty days to have sex increased the likelihood they would still be dating one year later. "There's more to a relationship than sex, but we did find that those who waited longer were happier with the sexual aspect of their relationship." Nearly one-quarter of those who waited thirty days were still together a year later. As for those who were quick to jump in bed, well, ninety percent of those couples didn't even make it one year. The evidence supports waiting until marriage, and it supports the fact that people who have the most sexual partners have the most unfulfilled marriages and relationships versus people who have had sex with only one partner. The waiters have the most fulfilling relationships, regardless of what the world tells you. The proof is out there; you just have to be willing to accept it and embrace it for yourself. You can find all the links to the videos and articles on the "W.W.W." website.

There's a parable in the Bible about a wise and foolish builder. The foolish builder built his house on sand, while the wise man built his house on stone (which I'm sure took longer). The parable says that when the storms came, the house built on sand fell with a thunderous crash. The house built on stone weathered the storm. If you have sex too soon and connect to someone you're not in love with, you are attempting to build a house on a foundation of sand. Sure, it will be faster and easier than waiting for that right person, no one likes digging a foundation; but don't start complaining later when things start falling apart in your relationship. Take the time on the front end to find out who that person is, and make sure you're ready for life with them before you jump into bed and into a relationship with them; thus, saving yourself so much more pain and wasted time on the back end. I've been through enough messy breakups that I don't want to get myself into something that's going to cause me or another person heartache when I can avoid it. Even if it means being lonely (and horny) while I wait for the right one. If you want a ride or die companion like that to go through life with and to be a ride or die partner for someone else, build a foundation on something more solid than the fact that they're good in the sack. Because when the storms of this life hit, and they will hit, you're going to need a lot more than reverse cowgirl to get through.

As much sex as we all like to think we're having, a small percentage of our lives is spent getting it on. In preparation for the short ad film "25,915 days" Reebok, in conjunction with global consultancy Censuswide, conducted a study to find out what we do with our time. In addition to discovering we only spend 180 days exercising they also found that the average person spends only 117 days of their life having sex. This makes up 0.45% of our lives. You have to live with that person the other 99.5% of the time! Choose someone you enjoy spending time with more than anything else.

The saddest situations I see, and the most common, are people who just wanted to have sex and never learned to control their sexual appetite and ended up stuck in a relationship with someone wrong for them. You see this happen all the time whether you are aware of it or not. The real risk here lies outside the obvious. Due to promiscuity, it's easy for individuals never to finish, or even start for that matter, what they were put on this earth to do because they didn't have the right person by their side to help them do it! This is one result of THE SEX TRAP.

CHAPTER FIVE
THE SEX TRAP

"I was up above it; Now I'm down in it."
Trent Reznor (Nine Inch Nails)

The male and female brains are wired very differently. As a result, having sex too quickly will usually end in one of two ways:

1) The woman will get attached, and the man will get cold feet, resulting in hurt feelings and a broken relationship (women, how often have you slept with a man who seemed "into you" before having sex; only to see him become distant after getting intimate? Right).

I can imagine a woman reading this and thinking, *No this isn't true.* Speaking from my experience, if a woman will have sex with you, she almost always wants to be in a committed relationship at some point. Eventually, this turns into waiting for a proposal ... you can see where I'm going.

2) The other thing that happens too often is the new couple continues to date and sleep together, and unless they get EXTREMELY lucky (on the level of someone who hit the lottery), they find themselves in a relationship with less than their ideal match.

When a couple has sex, oxytocin is released and can be mistaken for love. The sex did what it was designed to do; it connected them.

The pair thinks they are in love. But they hardly even know each other! Now they are bonded, emotionally, chemically, physically. Then they live not-so-happily ever after, wasting years of each other's lives, sometimes, wasting their entire lives! When the "sex trap" is full-blown, one person (if not both), often winds up losing physical attraction for the other (regardless of how good the other person looks); resulting in sexual desires for others instead of, or at least in addition to, their spouse. The one person is no longer enough.

Hear this; if you don't connect with your partner on a deep level, they won't be enough to satisfy you physically long-term. Yes, there is more to a relationship than sex, but a couple's sex life often reflects the state of their relationship. When couples stop having sex, start swinging, or one begins cheating, it is usually a symptom of being disconnected ... **finding out if you connect on a deep level takes time!** Hence, why waiting works.

Here's the kicker, in the long run, the couple that didn't pump the brakes winds up having less sex and being less fulfilled than the couple that exercised some self-restraint on the front end and waited to get to know the other person before bedding them. It's part of THE SEX TRAP, and it happens ALL THE TIME.

Talk about putting the cart before the horse! This is clearly ass-backward. I don't want to get stuck or have anyone stuck to me, whom I don't plan to be with for the long term. In my past, I never realized this or thought it all the way through and had to experience some hard lessons because of it. This explains why Lisa and some of my other former girlfriends would continue to stick around and put up with my shit; they got attached to me during sex. This also explains why even though I knew I wasn't in love and wanted to be free, I couldn't break up with them.

I'm no psychologist but seeing this pattern in my own life and talking to lots of other men and women, I came to realize how common this problem is.

When two people meet and go out on a date before ever really getting to know each other, if neither has a firm resolve to delay sex until marriage, there's a good chance they will wind up becoming another statistic. And once you're in it, it becomes hard to think and see clearly because SEX MASKS PROBLEMS.

SEX MASKS PROBLEMS

Let's face it; sex clouds our judgment. It just does. Have you ever been physical with someone and felt like you were in love, then in hindsight you were never in love? I'm going to go out on a limb here, and although I've never actually done it, I think most people would agree that getting married (choosing the person you will spend the rest of your life with!) is one of the most important decisions a person will ever make. All you need is to look at how ugly, drawn out, and expensive most divorces are to see this is true. So, my question is if you are going to make one of the most important decisions of your life, do you want clear judgment, or do you want a clouded perspective when making it?

It was 2011; my relationship with God and the work on myself I had neglected for years, was still there, waiting for me to get it together. At this time, I believed in Jesus, attended church somewhat regularly, and even tried to read my Bible on occasion. However, I was in a very backslidden state. Backslidden would be an understatement, but I was still holding on to God. I was distant from Him, but to be honest, I didn't know how to get back to Him. I would go to church on Sunday and watch people lift their hands in worship. I couldn't make myself feel the way they seemed to feel about God. I felt numb. I tried with everything in me to live the way I believed God wanted me to. Yet I failed miserably, so I figured I had blown my chance, and He was done with me. I continued sinning, which included sleeping with whatever girl I was dating at the time. I didn't know another way of doing life. I didn't see another option for becoming the man I wanted to be.

Camilla was my last girlfriend. Our relationship was rocky, to say the least. Over the year and a half we saw each other, we broke up no less than twenty times. But every time we broke up, a week or so would go by, and we would end up back together. We probably got back together due to the sex because the sex was good. She kept my interest more than any other girl I had dated up to that point, and oddly it was because I knew I couldn't trust her. That lack of trust kept me off balance. I caught her in little lies she would explain away. As my relationship with God improved so did my relationship with Camila. We started getting along better. I began to think maybe I was in love with her. I honestly didn't know, but for the first time, I thought it was possible.

As I grew closer to God, though I felt more and more like sleeping with Camila wasn't what He wanted. I felt the Holy Spirit's conviction. He wanted more of me. He expected obedience. Before, I justified having sex with Camilla because I had strong feelings for her. But as I grew closer to the Lord, a shift occurred. I don't know exactly when or how it happened. But my desire for obedience to God began to outgrow my desire for sex with Camilla. Still, I had legitimate fears. I distinctly remember thinking, *If you don't have sex with her, you will become a man-whore again, and that will be much worse. It's better to have sex with her than with multiple girls.* It was a reasonable argument considering my past. But despite the doubt in my head, I decided to obey, what I believed God was leading me to do and trust Him with the outcome. I now know the thought that I would fail was from the enemy, fear always comes from the enemy. Fear is never from God.

I sat down one day, and I had an honest conversation with God. I told Him I would try and do it His way. I told Him my fears and concerns, and I asked Him if I was in love with Camila to convince me, and I would marry her. But if I wasn't in love, convince me of that and break us up since we obviously couldn't do it ourselves. I felt a deep sense of peace come over me, ensuring me I made the right decision.

The next day I went over to Camila's house, and I sat her down to break the news. I said, "Look, I don't know if we are built to last. But I believe the way to find out is to stop having sex with each other." She didn't see eye to eye with me like I hoped, but she saw how serious I was, so she reluctantly agreed. I assured her if we both became convinced we were in love we would get married. I also added if we became convinced we weren't in love we should break up and stop wasting each other's time.

After dating for over a year and a half and having sex regularly, we cut the sex off. The first few weeks were the hardest. I was used to having sex whenever I felt like it, usually a couple times a week, and that appetite didn't just go away because I had decided to stop. A funny thing happened though, the decision to not hook up, and the subsequent marriage conversation between Camila and me that followed, began to give us clarity about the relationship. All the deeper issues we'd been ignoring came to the surface. I could see things more clearly and so could she. It was like the clouds parted, and for the first time, I was able to think and audit the relationship. Right around week three, I got a text from Camila letting me know she wanted to break up. I agreed.

That experience taught me a valuable lesson. There is no sense of urgency to evaluate your relationship when you are having sex. Why would you? You're meeting one another's basic, physical need, so the emotional and spiritual ones tend to get pushed to the side. You might wonder if you love them or if you could spend the rest of your life with them. You might even sense that something is missing. But you are never forced to examine the relationship. The decision to stop having sex, on the other hand, forces you to look at the relationship. It's basically like saying, "Well I want to have sex again, and I know you want to have sex again too. So, if our love is genuine, then let's get married. If it's not real, let's stop wasting each other's time!" We are all human, and sex is a deep, natural desire, so removing it from the relationship allows you to explore the connection you have, or think you have, with each other on an emotional, mental, and spiritual level.

Biology is behind this. We are human, and sex is a natural, deep desire. Not having sex puts the relationship under a microscope and allows you to examine it to see if it's going anywhere. No more one foot in, one foot out. Either you go both feet in by getting married or go both feet out and break up. It's an intentional move. Marriage forces you to, "shit or get off the pot," … "Fish or cut bait," as the sayings go.

When you stop having sex, you figure out whether you're really in love. Another reason why waiting works.

ARE YOU DATING MR./MS. RIGHT OR MR./MS. RIGHT NOW?

If you're reading this and are sexually active with your partner thinking "Well it's too late, this book doesn't apply to me," yes it does. There's still hope! If you want to audit the relationship to see if you are going anywhere (if the love is real), the best thing to do is have a conversation with your partner and intentionally cut off the sex. It provides ultimate clarity so you can decide on whether to start progressing toward marriage or cut your losses. I know this isn't an easy thing to do, but I'm telling you from experience it can be done, and it works.

Maybe you're in a relationship, and you're afraid the other person will break up with you if you cut it off. If they do, then I can tell you right now that they aren't the right person because they don't respect you or your values. Don't let fear stop you from doing the right thing. The oldest trick in the book the enemy uses against us is fear. If that person loves you, they won't leave. There's a saying that goes "If a man loves you nothing can keep them away. If he doesn't nothing can make them stay." The same is true for a woman. It's the quickest way to find out if what you have is real. It gives you ultimate clarity. Most people are afraid of being alone, so they forfeit the right path. The harsh reality is, you could waste years of each other's lives just having sex, causing you to miss your person.

* * * * * *

The most common red flags couples deal with like anger, jealousy, secrecy, insecurity, and immaturity are much easier to recognize in a potential mate when we're not in a physical relationship with them. You tolerate far less drama without sex. Once you become physical, you are prone to overlook things because you're attached to the other person via the cocktail of hormones pumping through your system. Some people take this kind of denial to an extreme by tolerating infidelity! Maybe you know a couple that fights all the time, and it's clear to everyone, except them, that they aren't right for each other. Maybe that is you. You sense something is missing. You are in love with *the idea* of being with someone although all the signs are telling you to *run Forrest run!*

I was that person. I wasted years having sex with girlfriends who were never going to be my wife because we couldn't get beyond a surface relationship. I was never in love with any of them. I had sex with them quickly, created a soul tie then overlooked the problems we had and stayed a lot longer than I ever should have. Did I care about my girlfriends? Sure. I had bonded enough to stay in a relationship with Lisa for five years! But I got stuck, I was not IN LOVE with her.

I know you're thinking this is radical! What would my friends think if I quit having sex? Consider this; your friends won't have to raise your out-of-wedlock child or contract an STD because you were worried about what people thought and had sex. As far as what your friends think, what do you care? You're not marrying them. You aren't going to be spending the rest of your life with them or building a family with them. If you want what your friends have, do what they do. If you want something different, you must do something different.

CHAPTER SIX
LUST vs. LOVE

"I don't believe in love at first sight. You fall in lust with what your eyes see, and in love with what your heart sees"
Unknown

Most people are familiar with the verse from Corinthians 13 that is popular in weddings that says love is patient and kind. Sex before commitment is impatient and demanding. It is about meeting my needs now. It's a cheap counterfeit for devotion. I heard lust defined once as, "I want what I want, and I want it now." Lust means using another person to satisfy an urge; it's like scratching an itch.

In relationships based on lust, one person is in control, and the other is in pursuit. The Controller is not as emotionally invested. The Controller calls the shots but quickly finds the relationship boring. The Pursuer experiences constant peaks and valleys. When the connection feels good, it's incredible! The Pursuer loves to be around the Controller. But when things aren't going well, the Pursuer is miserable and experiences a rollercoaster of emotions. I was the one in control, but bored. I stuck around longer than I should have because I had sex with all the women I dated and subsequently became bored. Inevitably, I fell into a kind of sex trap with all of them. Ultimately, it's the women who typically lose the most in these dynamics. Which is why I can't stress enough that you protect your hearts, ladies. You are its best guardian.

We all know love requires sacrifice. We see it in movies like "The Notebook." It is the favorite movie of every girl I know. Why? Because the sacrifice the man makes for his wife. Who doesn't want to be loved that way? Who doesn't want to love that way? Love bases its decisions on what's best for the other person. It's not self-centered.

I think the question we all need to begin asking ourselves before we jump into a physical relationship with another person is, am I ready to finish what I start here? That may be a premature question if you don't know the person, which is why I suggest getting to know people before sleeping with them. Why not get to know them and see what kind of person they are? Sex before marriage doesn't require any sacrifice because it's all about self-gratification. *Let's take them for a test spin to see if they tickle me right.* Do you see the difference here?

NO SEX BEFORE LOVE

Start talking about abstaining from sex before marriage and everyone freaks out. The idea sounds extreme to most. But if I were to say, "No sex before love," would that sound more reasonable? It's a thought we can get our heads around. The next question is, "How do you know if you're in love?" My answer would be that marriage, or the willingness to commit to someone is the ultimate proof of love. Few people will marry just so they can have sex. Most people believe when it comes to love it's best to follow your heart. Even when I talk to my single Christian friends who are sexually active about the idea of waiting until marriage to have sex, they will say, "Well God knows our heart." Yes, He does, and the Bible says, "the heart is deceitful above all things." (Jeremiah 17:9) This verse tells us that our hearts will deceive us into believing something that's not true, so we give our flesh what it wants. As John Bloom, the author of "Don't Follow Your Heart," describes it: "The truth is, no one lies to us more than our own hearts. They don't tell us the truth; they just tell us what we want. They are not benevolent; they are pathologically selfish. In fact, if we do what our hearts tell us to do, we will pervert and impoverish every desire, every beauty, every person, every wonder, and every joy. Our hearts want to consume these things for our own self-glory and self-indulgence."

Imagine you're dating someone, and you say, "I'm in love with you. Now let's have sex." And they say, "I'm in love with you too! Let's go get married first." Wouldn't you react like, "Whoa, hold up! Let me think about this a little longer?" Marriage feels like a more permanent arrangement because we know getting out of it is painful and difficult. So before having sex and getting into something complicated, we test our heart to see if it's telling us the truth. Marriage changes the conversation because we know it is the ultimate commitment and it would be painful to go through a divorce. The potential for marriage forces us to evaluate our feelings to see if we are indeed in love, so we don't get stuck with someone we aren't in love with and who, most likely, isn't in love with us! Commitment provides the perfect balance. As bad as I want to have sex, I equally as bad don't want to get divorced.

Loving someone in the good times is easy. We see the proposals, the engagements, the weddings, and the receptions, and it's all full of joy, as it should be. But life is hard. Life is real. Tests and trials will come. That is not the time to throw in the towel, but to step up to the plate! And my brother, my sister, if you married out of desperation, if you married because the sex is good, if you married because the clock is ticking, your day of reckoning will come. It is guaranteed to happen. It is imperative you use every weapon in your arsenal to choose and connect with the man or woman who will help you find and fulfill your purpose.

We must not be naive when it comes to marriage and the sacrifices required. We all want love. We all want that person who will stick with us through thick and thin. We want that person who will fight for us, defend us, encourage us, love us. The question isn't do we want to find that ever-lasting love because we all do. The question is, in my best Tim McGraw voice, how bad do you want it? If you want something real, if you want something of substance, something authentic; make the sacrifice to wait.

I saw a funny meme recently that said: "some people are marriage material, and some are mattress material." My female friends ask me all the time how they will know if a guy is serious about his interest in them or if he just wants sex. It's simple I tell them, if he is serious he will marry you.

* * * * * *

Envision yourself as a traveler looking for the perfect piece of land on which to settle down and build a home. As you set out, a wise older person gives you a bit of advice and says, "When you find the land you like, roll out a sleeping bag and get a feel for it, see if you want to spend the rest of your life there before you purchase it and build upon it. But whatever you do, don't pitch a tent! The danger is that once you pitch a tent, you will become comfortable there and may miss out on another piece of land that far exceeds all your hopes and dreams and would have made you happy for the rest of your life." I'm not comparing a person to land, but I think you get the analogy. So many times, in my past relationships, I "pitched a tent" before ever really feeling the other person out. I'd get comfortable and find myself in a place that I couldn't get out of. Not only was I unhappy, but I was incapable of making the other person happy because I couldn't love them the way they deserved to be loved. I wasted, not only years of their lives, but I wasted years of my life in pursuit of fake connections because of my lack of self-control.

PHYSICAL ATTRACTION FADES

One night as I undressed and started getting ready for bed, I was hoping my girlfriend wouldn't initiate sex. I told myself I was too tired to go a few rounds. *What is wrong with me?* I wondered. I was in my mid-thirties, not old enough to not want sex. Plus, my current girlfriend was an absolute

"10." I've dated some pretty girls but this one, we'll call her "Cheryl," was the hottest of them all. It was like God custom-made her for me.

With other girls I had dated, after a while I would begin to pick them apart physically. It happened subconsciously, but I remember my thoughts; *She's kind of short, Her arms could be more defined, Her hair is a little dry.* It's embarrassing to admit, but that is how shallow I was because I based my relationships with women on their bodies. Cheryl's body was unique. There was not one thing physically about that girl I did not like. Every feature about her face, her lips, the size of her thighs, every body part, all the way down to the length of her eyelashes, I mean EVERYTHING about that girl was exactly as I liked it. However, I was preparing for bed, hoping to avoid an argument because I wanted to go to sleep rather than have sex. The saddest part was that pattern was the norm for me. That was how I felt every night, not only with Cheryl but every other girl I had dated for any length of time.

* * * * * *

"Duty Sex" is no fun! But that is what my sex life would lapse into in all my relationships because I never waited. Talking to other men and women about this topic I have come to realize this is a pretty common problem.

There's a saying that goes, "Show me a beautiful woman, and I'll show you a man who's tired of F*king her." That quote is terrible and offensive. It angers most women. I get that. However, there's some truth to it. Look at Jay-Z and Beyoncé as an example. They are famous, rich, idolized, respected by many, and Beyoncé is gorgeous. But Jay-Z admitted to having an extra-marital affair. Instead of getting mad, let's try and figure out why this statement has merit.

Rather than writing cheating off as normal, let's see if we can get to the root of the problem. When people repeatedly cheat, they begin to think something is wrong with them. *Maybe I'm not meant to be with one person? or Are humans really meant to be monogamous?* These are some of the thoughts that crossed my mind as I began to examine the patterns in my previously failed relationships. I realized that every relationship I had ever been in started with sex on the first date or very early in the relationship. I recognized too, that because I had never taken a stance on waiting, I made choices about who to date almost solely from a physical standpoint. Knowing I was going to have sex sooner or later (ok sooner) caused me to make hasty decisions about the women I dated. I wasn't asking myself, "Is it even possible that this girl could be a good wife one day?" It was more like, "She's beautiful, and she doesn't look too crazy, so why not?" This is what happens, I believe for many of us.

When you're not committed to waiting until marriage (and by committed, I mean steadfastly committed), on some level, you will always let physical attraction dictate whom you date. Something deep inside of you will know that even if you don't marry the person, there will still be a payoff (sex) at some point. And when you make decisions based on only the physical, rather than evaluating people on a deeper level by trying to figure out who lives inside that shell (because that's all these bodies of ours are), you will get wrapped up with the wrong person. The odds of winning the lottery are probably better than finding your match going about it as everyone else does. It does happen, but the odds are stacked heavily against you, my friend. Why would you start your life with someone with the odds against you if you can help it?

Let's look at this honestly. Have you ever met someone and initially thought *wow they're hot!* but for whatever reason, you didn't date and just got to know them? Then after a little while, you look at them and still recognize they are attractive but think, *yeah, but not for me.* That happened because you broke through the surface to the underbelly of who they are.

The truth is the physical stuff is easy. We could be physically attracted to a lot of women/men. Now let's flip it around and say you asked this person out on a date before getting to know them. You sleep together after your third date (or sooner). Do you see now how people get stuck in relationships with the wrong people all the time?

I DON'T WANT YOUR SEX

One of the things single people hear married people say is "the sex stops after you get married." Unfortunately, statistics would seem to back this presumption. Only forty-eight percent of women say they still want regular sex after just four years of marriage.

This statistic comes from the Kinsey Report, a study into the sex lives of Americans by the National Centre for Health Statistics. This IS a problem! Sex is an important component to a successful relationship.

How many of us want a fifty percent chance of divorce and a fifty percent chance of having no sex in our marriage if we're one of the "lucky ones" that stay married? These are the odds folks, and like I said before "numbers don't lie." But I don't believe love fades away like that. Without a commitment (before sex) to put your heart to the test, it's almost impossible to know if you're really in love; it could just be the sex.

So, what am I suggesting? Instead of having sex stop after marriage have the sex *start* when you get married and have decades of great sex with a spouse who loves you and has committed to love you through thick and thin. Imagine how great your honeymoon will be because you built up an appetite for your bride or groom who you're deeply in love with. How sad when people have sex before they get married and deprive themselves of that experience. They completely miss out.

Imagine Thanksgiving dinner. You walk into your parents' house, and you smell the turkey cooking and see the stuffing, and you are hungry. Your mom announces that dinner will be ready in thirty minutes. But rather than wait you say, "I'll have a sandwich instead." The food comes out, and your appetite isn't nearly what it would've been had you waited, and therefore the food doesn't taste as good because of it.

Waiting until marriage to have sex lets your appetite build for your future lover. It also gives you valuable time, with complete clarity, to recognize any red flags that might make you call it off. You have the opportunity to think twice about spending the rest of your life with someone as you move closer to marriage. Be smart and do this *before* you get into a complicated physical relationship where you're not thinking so clearly.

Men especially need to look for something else in women besides beauty. Physical attraction is only a small part. After a while, it's less important. Beauty can be a trap, and many men fall into it. God made men visual, and he made women visually appealing to us. That beauty is what attracts a man, but it is her heart, her mind, and her soul that you will depend on when times are tough, and life knocks you around. It is her values that will influence your children and her morals that will keep her faithful to you when you're not as buff as you once were.

If we base our decision to allow someone into our personal life solely based on superficiality, we cannot be angry when their lack of character and substance become evident. Yes, she's sexy, with a coke bottle figure. Yes, he's fine with six-pack abs. But what about their character and their integrity? I challenge you to look for more because you will need more, as you walk through this life. And the only thing pre-marital sex can offer you is a clouded perspective.

YOUR HEAD CAN'T TELL YOUR HEART HOW TO FEEL

For most of my dating life, I had a mental checklist of what I was look-ing for in a woman. The list was something like; she had to be attractive, trustworthy, get along with my family, etc. I realized over time though that your head can't tell your heart how to feel; your heart either responds to someone, or it doesn't. Imagine being locked out of your house. You see a shiny silver key lying on the ground. It looks identical to the key to your home. You think, *this has to open my door!* But when you stick it in the lock, it doesn't fit. How can this be? It looks exactly like your key. The reason it doesn't work is that it takes a particular key to unlock your door. And it takes a certain kind of person to unlock your heart. There are so many intricacies in that lock that the key must be carved perfectly, meticulously, and purposefully, to open your door. As it should be with your heart. There must be substance and connection.

From a prudent standpoint, it makes sense to refrain from sex until the right person comes along. I tend to believe everyone has one right person for them. I can't prove it, so I won't even try to make the case.

But whether it's one person or one percent of the opposite sex that could make you happy long term, I don't believe it's any more than that. So just from a numbers standpoint, waiting to have sex is the smart way to go. Think about it, you may have to go through fifty or more people to get to that one person. If you have sex with all the people you date on the way to that one person; there's a pretty good chance you will get hemmed up with at least a few of them and never make it to your person.

Until you remove sex from the equation, and I believe this is the God's-honest truth, the chances of you finding that unique key are slim to none. Only when you draw your line in the sand and mean it, can you start to look at people with eyes that see past the physical and start looking for the person who will be right for you long term. Because if you aren't having sex until your wedding night, there's no point in even going on a date with someone unless you see that potential in them. Get it? I hate to make it sound this simple, but it takes so much of the complication out of dating and finding the right person. Once you remove sex before marriage from the table, the process of elimination begins to take over, and your odds go way up of finding your person because you're going through the duds very quickly.

CHAPTER SEVEN
TRANSFER OF CONTROL

"Men look for sex and find love.
Women look for love and find sex."
Unknown

Sex before marriage has become the norm in society. It's almost expected in every dating dynamic. I believe a woman can change the narrative when she realizes she has the power. If a man loves her, he will back it up by marrying her. I believe too many women are innately afraid to put their foot down and take that stance because they have become jaded. Women think *no one waits anymore* or *if I don't give it to him, another girl will.* They fear losing the guy and assume he will find someone else. That may be true, but that means that he didn't love them anyway, and they just saved themselves a bunch of time and heartache.

In my observations, when a woman has sex with a man who isn't in love with her, one of two things usually happens. The guy gets cold feet and bounces because he got what he wanted, which leaves the woman hurt and damaged; or she gets into a relationship with a man who doesn't satisfy her deeply and whom she can't satisfy deeply.

Here is where I typically find myself in some heated debates. Let me take it back to the beginning and boil relationships down to a base level, the way I believe God designed it. In relationships men and women want different things, *men want sex and women want security.* Therefore, each person's motives and what each brings to the table coming into it are completely different. Knowing this fact, what a man has control over, then, is when to give the commitment (marriage i.e., security) and what a woman has control over is when to give the physical (sex). If we did it the way God designed it, by waiting to have sex until marriage, we would be offering the other person what we had to give in return for what we were seeking at the right time. It's the perfect exchange, with the perfect timing, and it's what makes each of us happy long term. It's as if the man is saying through marriage "I will love you, provide for you, take care of you and give you all the security that comes with commitment if you will marry me give me your beauty, your body, and your respect." Please don't kill the messenger and be open-minded enough to test out this theory. Obviously, there is much more that men and women bring to the table, and there are exceptions to every rule. But, at our core men and women have relational needs that only the other can meet. It might sound sexist, but it's the truth whether you like it or not. I know today we like to make it out like both sexes are the same. While we are equal, we are not the same.

If a woman lies about how many partners she had is it usually less or more? Less, right? If a man lies about how many sexual partners he had, is it less or more? More, right? There's a reason for that. Prostitution is the world's oldest profession, and we all know who is selling what to whom. Trust me; women don't have to pay for sex. They can get it anytime they want. Any woman, even unattractive women, can have sex pretty much anytime they choose. Men do not have that option. Think about it, coming into a relationship 99 times out of 100 the woman says *when* they have sex. Most guys will take it as fast as a woman will give it.

Look at a man's body. Men are built for work. They are strong and by nature driven to produce and protect ... security. That's why men die of heart disease or attacks at such a high rate. We will literally work ourselves to death. Women are softer, more curvaceous, their bodies are more aesthetically pleasing … sex. There's a reason women wear makeup and high heels and shave their legs. I know some metro-sexual guys do but very rarely does a man spend as much time grooming as a woman. We don't even use the same words to describe a good-looking man versus a good-looking woman. A man is handsome, but a woman is *beautiful!* There's also a reason it is typical for men to pick up the tab on a date, hold open doors, and ask a woman to marry him. It might sound old-fashioned, but there is an undeniable truth here.

Society reminds of this truth through perversions of this dynamic with websites like SugarDaddy.com, AshelyMadison.com, and Arrangements.com, where wealthy men are looking to trade security (in this case money) for sex with younger women. Of course, when it's perverted, neither person finds what they're looking for, which is love and someone who cares about them whom they connect with on a deep level. Nonetheless, this is how God designed it. We've twisted it. All of this illustrates God's plan for marriage and gives us some clues as to how to approach dating.

If women understood the power they wield over men *before having sex* with them it would change the game dramatically. Before having sex, a woman has leverage over a man *who is interested in her*. Ladies need to realize that, recognize their value, and understand they are in control.

We are all selfish by nature. Guys will say and do just about anything to get sex without committing. Men who aren't committed to waiting will be charming, funny, spend money, be the perfect gentlemen, take you on trips, even lie and manipulate, ANYTHING to have their way and get unrestricted sex. But when a woman has sex before a commitment (and I mean real commitment, i.e. marriage), she gives her power away to someone who hasn't been clear about his intentions. So a woman who *gives sex* but doesn't *get security* in return is *giving* and not *getting*. A man who is *getting sex* but not *giving security* (commitment) is just *getting* and not *giving*.

Therefore, the world looks at a man who has sex with a lot of women as a stud. But a woman who has sex with a lot of men is considered a ho. I'm not saying that one is less guilty than the other, but can you see the difference here?

· · · · · ·

All throughout history men have spent money and fought wars, killed and died for women. They've written the most beautiful poetry and love songs for women they admired from afar. God created men to pursue, to chase, and to conquer. When a woman gives it up to a man who isn't her husband, she has given up the prize too easily, and the man's desire to keep pursuing her diminishes quickly. If a guy is interested in a woman, he will pursue her. He will swim the river and climb the mountain to get to her. If he's not, having sex with him will only keep him around for a little while, but it isn't going to make him love her. She'll have a guy who's one foot in and one foot out, and neither one will be truly fulfilled long-term. This dynamic happens all the time, and it is the opposite of waiting for the right person to come along who is willing to marry you.

One of the major problems I see is women have made it too easy on men, and they are *giving sex* without *getting security* (marriage) first. How many times have you seen women in physical relationships waiting for the commitment saying things like "Girl, I don't know when he's going to propose." Well, I'm sorry to tell you, but he's probably not in any rush. He's not motivated!

Many men will jump from woman to woman never committing if the women let them. Because commitment means responsibility, and if we can get the same benefits with none of the work required, we will. Ladies, it is your responsibility to make them commit.

If the women I dated had asked me to wait to have sex with them until we were married, this strategy would have worked on me, without question. Would I have waited to have sex with them and married them? Absolutely not. The reason it would have benefited them (and me) is that it would have weeded me out. At that time in my life, I was only looking for sex; I was not looking for a wife or even love to be honest. As a result of neither the women in my life nor me having strong boundaries in this area, we had good sex, but I was an awful boyfriend who cheated on them and broke their hearts. It's important women pay attention to what men say and *do*. Do not be blinded by his looks, education, money, or occupation. Men know women desire marriage. They'll bait you with words of affection and talk about *marriage and children* to captivate your attention to get you in bed. Sex is not love. Pay attention to words, but most importantly pay attention to actions.

TALK IS CHEAP

Another reason marriage works is that it forces us to put our money where our mouth is. There's a video of Mike Tyson where's he's in the ring with a guy named Bob Sapp. Sapp is talking smack like he wants to fight Tyson, and he calls him out. Tyson calmly smiles and steps up to the mic and says, "Sign the contract big boy, sign the contract." I love that clip because Tyson knew what I'm telling you here. Talk is cheap. A guy will say pretty much anything to get in a girl's pants. The sad part is, he might even mean what he says when he says it, but if a man can get a woman with just a few words and dinner, somewhere in his subconscious, she's become cheap to him. If he has to wait for her, if he has to "earn" her, she becomes much more valuable. Even if he can't articulate it, there is a part of a man that will view a woman who guards her purity as exceptional.

I see the provocative pictures women post on various social media sites, then they wonder why they attract the wrong type of guy. I can only speak for myself, but rather than attract, it repels me. Not that I find them unattractive or that I'm judging them, it's just that I am in a different place. I am looking for a wife and want to find love, so my desire is for more than just sex appeal. Do I want physical attraction? Absolutely! But there must be more. I want to tell those women, "You're using the wrong type of bait sister." The fish you want to catch don't bite on that. I'm not here to judge anyone, but I was the guy who sought out women who posted provocative pictures. These are the type of women bad guys feast on and throw away after they've consumed their hearts and souls. Today pictures like that repel and sadden me. I am no longer the man I once was. I think I can speak for the good men out there who desire more from a woman than just sex. We want substance. When a woman uses sex to attract a man, it speaks of her character and the type of man she's looking for. The same applies to men … watch how they carry themselves and pay attention to the image they present. Women and men all say they want a "good man or a good woman" without considering the image they portray to the world. You must be that good woman or man to get a good man or woman. The question to ask yourself isn't *is he or she the person I want?* But rather *am I the person the kind of person I want will want to be with?* That may sound convoluted, so I'll form it as a question: *Are you the person you're looking for is looking for?*

I have a friend who recently went through a divorce. He met a much younger woman and was excited about the prospects. He asked for my advice and if I thought it could work because of their age difference. He even talked to his kids about it to see how they felt. I told him I didn't know if it could work; but the way to find out if what he was feeling was real, was to decide not to have sex with her before marriage. This way he could get to know her better, outside of the bedroom and beyond just the physical attraction he was feeling for her. If he continued to feel this way and became convinced he was in love, then he could marry her and have all the sex he wanted.

Instead, they ended up having sex not long after our conversation. The next time I talked to my friend, I asked if he was still considering being with this girl and his reply was "Hell no! That was just a fantasy." The young girl wanted a relationship with him. But she lost any chance of that when she had sex with him because she gave her power away to a man who hadn't made any sort of promise to her.

Let's rewind the tape. Imagine the young woman had held out for marriage. They might not have sealed the deal, but they might have. He was thinking about a life with her before they had sex, he discussed it with his kids and me. There's always the possibility he would've realized she wasn't the right one for him anyway as they moved along and got to know each other. But that would've hurt her less than sleeping with him and hoping he'd like the sex enough to commit. Sadly, this is the typical pattern.

NO CHUPPY, NO SCHTUPPY

"There's a crude Yiddish expression that sums up the ancient sexual bargain between men and women: No chuppy, no schtuppy. It means, literally, no marriage, no sex."

In her blog, "The Sex Trap: Why Women Should Never Say Yes Before Marriage," Danielle Crittenden writes, "We may smirk at its primness, but as women, even as liberated, sexually uninhibited women, we still know exactly what it means. Men and women, by the very nature of their biology, have different, and often opposing, sexual agendas. Eventually, most women want children and, with them, a committed husband and father. Yet so long as there is no readily understood and accepted way for women to say no to men they like, and they hope to see again, women lose their power to demand commitment from men."

* * * * * *

The argument I hear most from men for engaging in sex early in a relationship is that you must test out your sexual compatibility. I don't know how many times that I've heard my guy friends say, "You wouldn't buy a car without taking it for a test drive." And yes, you're right, I wouldn't buy without taking it for a test drive, but women aren't cars.

Comparing a living, breathing human being to an inanimate object is stupid in the first place. But since people do it all the time, let's go with it. When a woman is a virgin she has a natural seal, it's called a hymen. Men who use this argument are saying they want to crack the seal and give it a try. Then if they don't like it, they can put the lid back on the rack and move on to the next item. What if we did this with products in the grocery store? Would it raise or lower their value? Do you want to buy milk someone else has sampled? You can see the stupidity in this argument, and how it breaks down if you take a moment to think it through. It doesn't work!

Ladies … do you want a man to invest his heart, his fortune, and his life to the level of your value? Then save yourself for him. If you are giving it away, you are lowering the value. There isn't one thing in all the world you can give away and raise its value. So why do we think that it's any different with our bodies?

Plus, if the theory of testing out sexual compatibility were true, the people who do not test it out would have shorter, more unfulfilling relationships. The problem with this is none of the research backs it up. The truth is people who have sex early on do not stay together longer. In fact, *they break up earlier, at a higher rate,* and are *less sexually fulfilled* in their relationships. (See the Resources page of the whywaitingworks. com for articles and studies relating to this.)

Another reason abstaining until a man proves his love for you by marrying you is sensible is because men aren't as worried about the time aspect. Men don't have a ticking biological clock. We can father children a lot later in life than women can become mothers. It's not uncommon to see older men who are easily able to pick up younger women. How often has the "Sexiest Man Alive" been a male actor well past mid-life? George Clooney is fifty-seven years old. His wife is almost twenty years younger, and they just had twins. Charlie Chaplin fathered children into his seventies; his last wife was thirty-six years younger. In The Rules Revisited, blogger "Andrew," writes "Don't give a guy your most eligible years with nothing to show for it. This is bullshit. If you ultimately want to get married and your current relationship isn't constantly growing stronger (i.e. approaching something permanent), then you need to start asking questions. And if you aren't getting satisfactory answers, it is time to look elsewhere. The clock is ticking."

THE MORE THEY PAY, THE LONGER THEY STAY

We used to have a saying when I promoted clubs that went like this: "the more they pay, the longer they stay," referring to the higher the cover charge to get in the club, the longer people would stay even if the place wasn't that crowded. Typically, we would charge ten dollars, and that was enough of a commitment for most people not to leave and go club-hopping. For events like the New Year's Eve party I throw every year, we charge $100-$150 to get in; no one leaves. Of course, it's all-inclusive, and it really is the best party in town, but still, the principle stands true. I think there's a lot we can learn from this when it comes to sex and dating.

I've now been abstinent for my second six-year stretch (Side note: I did make a mistake one night three years ago with a girl I'm close to, and it damn near cost me a friend). But aside from that one time, I haven't had sex in six years. If tomorrow, I meet my soul mate the amount of time I estimate we will date before getting married would be a year. So, if you add it up, at that point, I will have had seven years of abstinence under my belt. Now, suppose my wife and I get into an argument, how quickly do you think I'm going to walk away from that relationship knowing I may have to wait another seven years before meeting the next Mrs. Right and being able to have a physical relationship with her? Whatever happens in my relationship, we will work that out because I've waited a long time for her. I've abstained for her.

Contrast that with the national average of couples that waited three dates to have sex. How much easier is it for them to throw away the relationship at the first sign of trouble and find another person and start over if things go south?

Unfortunately, we are surrounded by oversexed people, and we live in a culture that tells us not to wait for anything. But is it better? Don't you usually appreciate the things you have to work for and wait for?

Peter Wentz of Fall Out Boy shared this amazing analogy, "Girls are like apples … the best ones are at the top of the trees. The boys don't want to reach for the good ones because they are afraid of falling and getting hurt. Instead, they just get the rotten apples that are on the ground that aren't as good, but easy. So, the apples at the top think there is something wrong with them, when, in reality, they are amazing. They just have to wait for the right boy to come along, the one who's brave enough to climb all the way to the top of the tree ...." Be the top apple, girl.

It requires a level of faith in the process and a firm belief in your worth, if not God. You can't force a man to commit per se, but you can force him to choose; either wait and commit or leave. I think too often women fear taking a stand and losing a man, so she compromises and settles for Mr. Right Now, rather than holding out for Mr. Right.

When I was the old me, it was easy to spot girls who didn't have high self-esteem. They were willing to sleep with me quickly. It was these same girls who wondered why they could never find a decent guy. I know where I'm at now and when I meet women who have taken a stand in that area, it is EXTREMELY attractive. A pretty face and nice body don't determine self-worth, attitude and actions do.

Women, spend less time working on the outside and devote more time to working on the inside. The Bible says, "Like a gold ring in a pig's nose is a beautiful woman who lacks discretion." Proverbs 11:22. The Rob translation of that verse is "Ladies you might be hot, but if anyone can get it, it ain't worth much." Guys want a prize. You are a prize! Act like it. Strive to be a woman of virtue with high standards. The Bible says it best, "Don't give holy things to dogs, and don't throw your pearls in front of pigs. They will stomp on the pearls, then turn around and attack you." (Matthew 7:6) A guy who desires only to sleep with you, and not marry you is considered a dog and a pig! Let that sink in. God says what you have to offer is holy ... your sex, your heart, your time ... is holy. When you decide to have sex with a man, you are giving him the most powerful, the most important, the most precious thing you possess. So be careful to whom you give your "pearls." You deserve the best man to accompany you through this life. Do not settle.

MEN DON'T HAVE COMMITMENT PROBLEMS

I have women friends who are sleeping with men who won't make the relationship official or who won't propose. They complain about those men's *commitment problems*. Let me set the record straight here; men don't have issues with commitment. Men commit all the time to the things that we want badly enough. I'll say it again, one of the biggest problems I see is that women are making it too easy on men and not making them commit.

The truth is he either doesn't like you enough to commit, or you are giving him all the luxuries of commitment with none of the requirements. It's *your right* to compel him to commit by not getting physical with him until he's ready to put up or shut up. As I have said before, do not give control of yourself over to a man who isn't willing to prove his love for you by committing his life to you. And I don't mean a Facebook status that can change with the click of a button. Women, you don't *ask* a man to commit, you quietly *demand it* with your actions. Then he will happily come along to get the sex, confident he has won the prize other men surely wanted but couldn't have. Get it? Otherwise, he'll assume the mindset of "let's just see how this plays out." When I promoted nightclubs the cover charge wasn't negotiable. You paid, or you didn't get in. It was that simple. Do not pass go, and do not collect $200. If we had allowed people in just to look around and check the place out, it would have been a revolving door. Ladies, please don't let men in so easily and then wonder why they don't stay.

Love Biologist, Dawn Maslar, M.S. describes an interesting conversation she had with her grandmother in the Ted Talk "How Your Brain Falls in Love" that went like this:

"My then 95-year old grandmother spoke up and she said, 'You youngsters don't know anything about love!'

"She said, 'Your problem is you young girls jump into bed too quick. You fall in love, but a boy doesn't fall in love that way.'

"And I kind of looked at her, and I said, 'OK, let's talk a little bit more: how does a boy fall in love?'

"And she said, 'Back in my day, a girl knew if she wanted a boy to fall in love with [her], she couldn't sleep with him right away.'

"I decided to continue with my grandmother, I said, 'How long do you need to wait before you have sex?'

"She says, 'Ah, you wait to have sex, until he falls in love.'

"'OK, well, granny, how do I know when he falls in love?'

"She says, 'Ah, that's easy. You know he's in love when he commits."

She continued to explain how the brains of men and women are dissimilar and as a result, how we fall in love differently: "Women take a bigger risk and tend to fall in love when they have sex, and men tend to fall in love when they commit."

This is why I say there is a transfer of power when a woman has sex with a man before marriage. A woman becomes biologically and emotionally invested the moment she has sex with him. Therefore, having sex pre-commitment can be very dangerous for a woman because essentially, she is giving control of herself and her emotions to someone who hasn't proven himself worthy of her trust. I know I keep harping on this, but it is crucial women get this. You are giving him one of the most precious gifts you have to give to someone who may not give one damn about you, and I want to implore you not to do it.

By design, women are more emotional. They get attached quicker, especially when they have sex. This, too, is why men can "hit it and quit it" easier than a woman. I'm sorry ladies, but it's true. I've heard women say they can have casual sex … it doesn't mean anything to them. Any woman who says that is either in denial or knows she's lying, and at some point, it will catch up with her. It's biologically impossible. The exception is when a woman has sex with so many different partners her emotional attachment through sex becomes void. It's as if her brain has literally been rewired and does not expect love, affection, or tenderness. I am not a misogynist by any means. My heart's desire and my goal are to help women protect their hearts and health.

You are not equipped with the ability to have sex with multiple people without suffering serious emotional and spiritual ramifications. Men reap their own consequences, they just manifest much differently. I will get to the men in the next chapter.

* * * * * *

In an article in Psychology Today, Rita Watson MPH says, "After making love, a woman might mistake the oxytocin release for feelings that tell her, 'this is your perfect partner.'"

Dr. Loretta Breuning, professor emerita at California State University, says: "Despite those initial feelings, it does not necessarily mean the person is trustworthy. The perception you have now is an illusion you create about the person that may or may not fit what happens next."

That illusion blinds women into believing a man is who SHE thinks he is, which could be completely different from reality. When choosing a mate for life women need all their faculties and emotions working on their behalf. No woman wants to look back in a decade or more and think, "I would give anything to go back and have a clearer picture of who this man really was." Having that clear picture is possible, but women must be their own best friend in a relationship and protect their most precious part, their heart. One way to guard your heart, ladies, is to guard your purity. You choose who you invite into your life. You also choose who you invite into your bed. These are choices you make. Therefore, you are responsible for the outcome of your choices, whether good or bad.

I love this quote by Hal Elrod, "The moment you accept responsibility for everything in your life is the moment you can change anything in your life." It is up to you to make sure you get the best life has to offer.

CHAPTER EIGHT
BECOMING A MAN

"When I was a child, I talked like a child; I thought like a
child; and I reasoned like a child. When I became a man,
I put the ways of childhood behind me."
1 Corinthians 13:11

Until now, I've put a lot of the responsibility on women for stopping the
madness of the current dating and sex scene. I'd like to shift my focus
and speak to men. Guys, here it is: It's time to grow up! Stop acting like
frat boys and start treating women with the respect they deserve.

Society tells us if we bed a lot of women we are a man. As if we must
conquer women to validate ourselves. A real man is one who protects the
women around him and can exercise self-restraint in the face of temptation. A real man adds value to other human beings; he is a guardian,
a warrior. Anyone can get laid and continue perpetuating the madness.
We need more heroes. I think of the verse, "When I was a child, I talked
like a child, I thought like a child, I reasoned like a child. When I became
a man, I put the ways of childhood behind me." (I Corinthians 13:11)

When did we as men stop protecting our women? More importantly,
why did we stop protecting our women? Ask any woman what qualities

they are looking for in a man, and I guarantee most of them will say they want a strong man of integrity who will lead them and their family. We are leading, but we're leading them astray. Not all men, but certainly a majority. If we want to change the narrative, we can. Not all men are dogs. We just need more men of integrity to lead the way, to stand up and show other men what integrity looks like. I know they are out there. I know there are guys looking for something deeper than meaningless sex who are willing to wait for the real thing. Where are the men willing to be one of the ones who will say no to sex, even when it's offered with no strings attached? It takes strength and maturity to deny that part of your nature. But it's what real men do. It takes integrity, sacrifice, and some lonely nights to exemplify what a real man is to other men, to the boys (like I was) who need a strong role model, and to women who want to believe in us again. Boys want what they want when they want it. Men have learned the value of patience and exercise self-control.

Men, these are our women, and it is OUR RESPONSIBILITY to treat them like the prizes they are. Otherwise, you are just contributing to the problem and to a broken system, and we all suffer. Grow up! Be willing to stand for something even if it costs you to do it. Everything worth having will cost you. A leader does what is right, even if it's unpopular or people call them crazy. You will never influence the world trying to be like the world. Fitting in means you blend into the background. You want a woman of substance and character, then be a man of substance and character. I know many men that believe they are a good person in their heart and then make excuses for their bad behavior. I love the quote in Batman Begins where Rachel says to Bruce Wayne, "It's not who you are underneath. It's what you do that defines you."

GOD'S DAUGHTERS

For those reading this who believe in God or some higher power, imagine how God thinks about His daughters. By establishing healthy parameters around sex, namely marriage, God is essentially saying "No, you don't get to sleep with my daughter unless you commit to take care of her, sacrifice for her, and promise to be around for a lifetime."

The Bible instructs us to treat younger women as sisters with absolute purity (I Timothy 5:2). The Bible also instructs husbands to, "Love your wives as Christ loved the church." (Ephesians 5:25) Are we really treating women as sisters? Men, are you loving your wives, or your future wife, as Christ loved the church? Jesus died for the Church! I aim to be the kind of guy that future husbands of my girlfriends will thank for helping them cross the finish line to make it to them. *Thank you for helping my wife navigate her way to the altar, and to me.* How do we do that? It starts by taking the focus off ourselves and beginning to look at the other person's needs.

THE GOLDEN RULE

When I talk about my faith, there's always someone who wants to tell me that "all religions are the same" and that they all essentially teach some version of, "do to others what you want them to do to you." That seems to be the one thing we can all agree on, religious or not, right? It's *the Golden Rule.* Jesus used it in Matthew to summarize Jewish law. Since we can all agree that is something to aspire to, and the world would be a better place if we applied that rule, here's my question, *are you doing that?* I mean *really* doing that?

I have friends of many different faiths who are devout. But too often they're not so faithful when it comes to sex outside of marriage. I know guys who go to church every Sunday and wear Jesus T-shirts, watch Christian movies, and are critical of people who drink, smoke, or cuss. But they're sleeping with their girlfriends.

So, guys, I'll ask you, "Are you treating that girl you are dating or talking to the way you would want your sister, your daughter, or your mother to be treated?" Because guess what ... they are that to someone. And if you are a Christian then you know the command Jesus gave us. If you are "loving your neighbor as you love yourself" that includes that girls' mom or dad, sibling or child. They are YOUR NEIGHBOR.

* * * * * *

By no longer being a scumbag and bedding any woman I could as fast as she would let me, I began showing respect and honor not only to that woman; but to every other person in her life who cared about her.

Every time I had sex with a girl in the past, deep down on some level, I knew that I was having sex with someone's future wife. Not a great way to "love your neighbor as you love yourself." Guys, if you're sleeping with a girl, and you're unsure whether you're going to be with her for the long term, (and if you haven't proposed, there's a good chance it's because you're not sure), then this is exactly what you are doing. Remember that every girl you date is someone's wife. At some point, she is going to marry someone. If it's not you, and you have sex with her, you are sleeping with another man's wife.

Have you ever had a problem with the ex of someone you were dating? I have. Because sex is so much more than just a physical act. I, for one, wouldn't want to walk into an establishment and be faced with five guys the girl I'm dating or married to had slept with. Deep down, I think it's because we know they took something that didn't belong to them. I'll put it like this. *If I'm willing to put a ring on her finger and make her my wife; why did you get the goodies when you weren't willing to man up?*

That's a question I wrestled with before in previous relationships even while I did the same thing. At some point, I had to recognize that, even as messed up as the world is, I was a part of the problem. I had to stop contributing to the problem and start being part of the solution. Even if I were the only person who chose to start doing things the right way it still mattered. And it matters for you.

Somewhere deep inside we wonder if that guy knows we slept with his girl. It's like this secret between her and you that is embarrassing. How many television shows and movies have we seen where there is some major conflict between partners over someone the other has slept with? If sex before marriage isn't wrong, then why are we embarrassed by who and how many people we've slept with? We tend to leave out details about our sexual past to try and make ourselves appear less of a horn-dog than we may have been, right?

I don't have children. But I can't imagine how protective I will be if I ever have a daughter, knowing how I was and how too many men think. I will probably buy a gun and keep a shovel in my trunk when she starts to date. Now when I meet one of my current women friend's father's and give him a firm handshake, look him in his eye and tell him what a great daughter he has, it's so much better than the feeling any amount of sex can provide. Or the feeling I get when I go to a girl friend's wedding and see her walk down the aisle knowing I had some small part in helping to navigate her successfully to a man who is ready to love, honor, and cherish her. There is no comparison. To think I traded that feeling for all those years for meaningless sex! What a stupid thing to do. Yes, women are the ones who are supposed to have discretion. But men it is our responsibility to model what a real man looks like and show the ladies there still are leaders willing to take a stand and do what's right. Even if a woman offers you sex, be smart enough to resist. Treat that woman like you would hope a man would treat your sister or mother and help her see her worth.

Fellas, straighten your back and be the man you were called to be, and let's live a life of integrity and discipline and honor the women in our lives as well as the women who have yet to enter our lives. Every woman who crosses your path isn't meant to be our wife. Some women need to see a man of integrity modeled for them. That may be your role in the lives of most of the women you know. I challenge you, to help mend women's hearts through friendship and honor. Good men need to remind women that chivalry still exists. I cannot rectify the wrong I've done in my past. But I pledge to exemplify what a good man looks like daily to the women in my life, and should you choose to do it too, you will thank me.

OBEDIENCE IS BETTER THAN SACRIFICE

Right now, in our society, volunteering has become trendy. I see celebrities, politicians, businesses, and close friends giving back and doing good in the community. I applaud those efforts. The world needs more people lending a helping hand.

Why not take those positive efforts a step further? Instead of talking about how much you're doing and receiving praise and accolades, consider this: *stop creating problems!* Because sex before marriage creates problems. Even if you just look at it on a purely base level, sex before marriage has caused many adverse social effects such as abortion, STDs, single-parent homes, loveless relationships, heartache, drama, conflict, etc.

There's a verse in the Bible that states, "Obedience is better than sacrifice." (I Samuel 15:22) It means that obedience to God is better than doing things that we would consider a sacrifice. I believe it's because obedience is harder. Obedience costs us more than sacrifice, and ultimately obedience leads to a better life. God doesn't demand our obedience because He wants to punish us or rob us of fun. He wants the absolute best for us, and because He made us He knows what that best is. His plan is always better.

With volunteering, we receive an immediate payoff. We feel great, knowing we've served our community, as we should. The sacrifice of our time and talents are typically met with praise and pats on the back. Obedience, on the other hand, doesn't feel good most of the time. It is usually counter-cultural. Obedience to God often opposes what society deems as the norm. Would you rather look good to people or God? I'll take the latter, thank you. There will always be tension between your desires and what you know is the right thing to do. For instance, if a single man and a woman decide to have sex, society would deem that as normal, positive interaction because both parties consented. Even though that is typical, an internal war may begin because you know instinctively that God expects more. You have free will, so the choice is yours, but obedience has a payoff. You may never know what that act of obedience could have helped you to avoid. Obedience will cause frustration. Obedience will require discipline. People may call you stupid. You may even feel stupid.

Either way, there are consequences for obedience and disobedience. The difference is obedience doesn't cause regret and shame. How many men have had sex with a woman only to want her to leave immediately afterward? Remember those awkward conversations after the fun was over? The thoughts about how to get out of there as quickly as possible without being completely rude? How many women have you left feeling used after you departed? How many women have never heard back from you after having the one-night stand? How about the woman you got pregnant and now fight with about child support, lack of quality time with your child, or just the struggles of being a single father?

Men also experience negative consequences of having a child out of wedlock, and they can be as emotionally and mentally taxing as they are for women. This isn't a book about parenting, or how a child needs a mother and a father in the home at the same time, fulfilling the roles God meant for them within a family unit. So, I'll focus on the men here: being a single father is damn hard! Men are not nurturing by nature and having to raise your child or children without their mother can leave you feeling inadequate and defeated. If you aren't ready to be a daddy, don't do what it takes to become one, because it is the hardest job in the world, and you will need a woman to help you do it right, men.

Be honest with her and tell her up front you aren't looking for a relationship, say you're not ready, that you've been hurt before, whatever! It doesn't matter what you SAY to a woman, she will catch feelings after sex. Then regardless of what you said, you will be the asshole and you will lose her as a friend (in addition to all her friends and family) if you slept with her before you were ready to commit to her. Do what it takes to keep yourself from making a mistake you and she will regret.

According to the US Department of Health sixty-four percent of youth suicides are from fatherless homes. Ninety percent of all homeless and runaway children are from fatherless homes; that is thirty-two times the national average. Eighty percent of rapists with anger problems came from fatherless homes. Men, we have dropped the ball here. We are planting our seeds randomly wherever we can, and we are reaping a generation of damaged people because of our selfishness and disobedience. It is time we grew up and became the men God intended us to be.

* * * * * *

The young lady or man who waits until marriage can potentially avoid all the negative scenarios we see play out every day. There may be frustration in the wait, and some of us must wait longer than others. But it will be worth it, and here's the real kicker, if we were obedient we wouldn't need sacrifice. Sacrifice is necessary because a problem exists; obedience prevents the problem from occurring in the first place. Remember those movies where the drug dealer is giving out turkeys on Thanksgiving? Yes, he's making a monetary sacrifice providing free turkeys and looks like a hero. But he's also poisoning the people in the neighborhood by selling them drugs. If you want to make the world a better place, stop creating problems for other people to clean up. Clean up your own mess.

As you start walking the path of purity, God has a funny way of honoring that commitment by giving you a clearer vision for your life and greater clarity. God honors obedience. Think about it. When did Adam and Eve's lives get hard? It was after they disobeyed. God said, "By the sweat of your brow, you will eat your food until you return to the ground." Until they sinned life was comfortable, and they enjoyed their work. We are all the children of Adam and Eve. So, unfortunately, we have to live with the sin they invited into the world. Thus, we need God's help and His hand on us as we navigate life. As I started to walk in obedience, I began seeing God's plan for me more clearly. It seemed too big and impossible to do on my own. I knew I needed to not only work very hard, but I needed Him to show up and make things happen that I had no power to make happen on my own. I reasoned that if I wanted God's help, I needed to do everything in my power to get sin out of my life, so there was no obstacle between Him and me.

There's a verse in the Bible where Job says he, "made a covenant with his eyes not to look lustfully at a young woman." A covenant is a promise to God that invites consequences. Covenants are good if you keep them and bad if you don't. What a scary thought. After rededicating myself and committing to purity, I was still regularly making mistakes in this area, albeit alone. I couldn't figure out what to do to stop it.

I came across a great article by Bob Sorge entitled, "Why You Should Make A Covenant With Your Eyes." In it, he writes why purity is essential to reaching our full potential and how making a covenant with God in this area provides the gas and the brake: "The eye," he says, "is the primary gate to our sexuality. Just as the gate in ancient cities regulated all incoming and outgoing traffic, our eyes determine the nature of the traffic that goes into and out of our hearts. Only when our eye gate is sealed from tempting sights can we find and hold the high ground of purity ... Picture your life as a car. To be operational, a car needs both a gas pedal and brake pedal. The gas pedal is the love of Christ, which propels you forward into purity. The brake pedal is the fear of the Lord, which stops you from crashing into compromise ...The pure heart, empowered by an eye covenant, will one day see God. Love catapults the heart into purity because it knows that purity gains the greatest of all possessions: God Himself ... We make the covenant because we want the fear of the Lord. We know we can't fulfill it in the strength of our natural will-power. It will require divine grace at every step. When you realize you're vowing something you cannot possibly perform in your flesh, it makes you tremble all the way through."

I decided to make a covenant with God. I wrote it out, dated it and signed it at the bottom. In the covenant, I made a pact with God not to "look lustfully or hold a lustful thought in my head intentionally." I confessed to God how weak I was in this area and asked Him to help me fulfill my vow. I asked Him to "bless me greatly and open doors for me that no man could shut," if I kept this covenant." I also asked Him to "punish me severely" and invited Jesus to "fight against me with the sword of His mouth" if I broke the covenant. Talk about terrifying. But that was and is my level of commitment. This is the gas and the brake. You want the blessing, and you fear the punishment. If this is something you would be interested in doing, I would recommend starting small, maybe commit to one day at first.

My covenant with God helped me break some strongholds in my life. At first, I started with just one day, then two, then three, then a week, a month and I got all the way up to six months. I've done several now, and I'd like to say I'm batting a thousand and have never failed, but I can't. I messed up a time or two. But I will say I saw God show up in incredible ways when I started this, and it gave me clarity in areas I didn't see before.

WHAT A MAN NEEDS

In 2004 a book began circulating that made an impact on a lot of marriages. It was titled "Love and Respect" and written by Emerson Eggerichs. His premise is that while women need love most, men need respect most. It was revolutionary because so many men are hesitant to admit they'd rather be respected than loved, and because so many women had never heard that. "Husbands are made to be respected, want respect, and expect respect."

Men, if you want to be respected by a woman, you must love and cherish her. When you honor a woman and put her first, she will respect you. Eggerichs wrote the book for marriage, but the principle applies to a woman you are interested in and may think you could marry. Your opinion and treatment of her have an effect on how she views herself and in turn on her opinion of you. He says, "The typical wife ... fails to realize that her self-image often rests on what she believes her husband thinks of her." Imagine that; a woman's self-esteem is largely based on her husband's view of her, or how she thinks he views her.

Even though my book isn't for married men, it is for men who will one day be husbands, and there is a lot to be learned from what he tells us. From a selfish standpoint what Eggerichs is saying is if you want respect from the woman you want you must first honor and love her. There is nothing honorable in trying to get into the panties of a woman you haven't committed to, and even if she can't articulate it she will feel dishonored and unloved, and she will not respect you.

CHAPTER NINE
GOOD THINGS COME TO THOSE WHO WAIT

"No discipline seems pleasant at the time, but painful.
Later on, however, it produces a harvest of righteousness
and peace for those who have been trained by it."
Hebrews 12:11

There's a timeless principle equated with having success in any and every area of your life. That principle is one known as delayed gratification. It's a common theme in success books, and we all recognize it to be true in just about every other area of our lives. Everything from getting in great physical shape to saving to buy a home, to climbing the corporate ladder, to getting our dream job. Whatever it is you are after there is one thing for certain … good things come to those who wait.

DELAYED GRATIFICATION DEFINED:
Delayed Gratification means making a choice that limits the ability of getting something now, for the pleasure of being able to have something bigger or better later. Or, I like the way Wikipedia defines it: the ability

to resist a smaller but more immediate reward to receive a larger or more enduring reward later.

DON'T EAT THE STEW

There's a story in the Bible about two brothers named Jacob and Esau. Jacob was the younger brother, and one day when his older brother, Esau, was hungry Jacob swindled Esau out of his birthright for a bowl of stew. Later in the Bible, Paul, the writer of Hebrews references sex outside of the confines of marriage to that story. The writer says no one should be "sexually immoral" or Godless like Esau who traded his birthright for a bowl of stew." (Hebrews 12:16)

The first time I read this, I was like, "Why in the hell would Paul be comparing sex before marriage to the story of Jacob and Esau?" But the more I thought about it, the more I understood it. Imagine the scene, Esau comes in after a long day of sheepherding, or whatever they did back then, and he is starving. His brother has something cooking on the stove, and it smells amazing! He wants it. He needs it. He must have it. So, he asks for some, and his brother says, "Sure you can have some, just trade me your birthright." Esau, like a dumb animal, agrees. There's a life lesson we can extract from the story of Jacob and Esau.

How long did that bowl of stew satisfy Esau? A few hours, a half a day max? And then guess what? *He was hungry again!* His birthright, on the other hand, would have satisfied him his whole life. It would've been a blessing to him until the day he died. But he traded it for something that only satisfied him temporarily because he couldn't wait. He forfeited houses, land, money, livestock because he never learned to control his appetite and therefore lost his long-term blessing.

I liken the birthright story to the woman God has for us. The woman God created to help us fulfill our ultimate purpose. He doesn't always send her right away. Sometimes we must wait for her and decline the numerous offers for stew we receive while we wait. Then one day, the perfect bowl of stew with all the right ingredients needed to fulfill us is presented. Too often, we pull up a chair at Golden Corral, when God wants to treat us to dinner at Fogo de Chao. My favorite definition of "failure" is giving up what you want most for what you want right now. The story of Jacob and Esau is a perfect example of that. How often do we trade what we want most, for what we want right now when it comes to sex and relationships?

MARSHMALLOW TEST

Delayed Gratification is best explained in a study conducted by Stanford Professor Walter Mischel. During the study, he left a group of children four to six years of age in a room alone with a marshmallow while he ran to do a quick task. He told the children that if they could wait fifteen minutes, they could have two marshmallows when he returned. Some children were able to wait the fifteen minutes, but most were not. In fact, most of the children ate the marshmallow the moment the professor walked out of the room! What's more interesting than this is that when they interviewed the same kids fourteen years later, they found the ones that were able to wait the fifteen minutes were more dependable, self-motivated, and had achieved significantly better grades throughout high-school, with no exceptions.

Further studies revealed that the children who were able to delay eating the first marshmallow scored higher SAT scores and had a lower BMI (body mass index) thirty years later! Not only did they fare better academically, earn more money, and were healthier and happier, they avoided adverse outcomes such as jail time, obesity and drug use.

So, are you a marshmallow now or a marshmallow later person? I was always the kid that ate the marshmallow as soon as the nice man walked out of the room. I assumed if there were another marshmallow in the future I would figure out a way to get that one later.

This study reveals a few things, namely that delaying gratification is a choice. Self-control is like a muscle that can be exercised over time. As you make good choices, it gets stronger, and your willpower is strengthened to say no to things that may be holding you back from your long-term goals, those things you want most in life. Mastering self-control enables us to be slaves to our appetites and desires no longer. It can start small and grow over time. We have a saying in the gym that refers to strength when lifting weights, *use it or lose it.* The more you use a muscle, the stronger it will get. If you don't exercise it, the strength you have built up will diminish. Avoiding something once will help you develop the skills to resist other temptations in the future.

INSTANT GRATIFICATION

Instant gratification, on the other hand, never produces long-term happiness. I often say the real-life punch line for instant gratification is Charlie Sheen. Once a great actor with a lifestyle that was envied by many men, he is now a shell of his former self. *Later on,* comes folks. You decide now what your future looks like. When we use sex as a form of escape, it's like using drugs in many ways. I know that's how I used it for much of my life. The only problem with using sex, or substances for that matter, as a form of escape, is when you come back to reality it's often worse than when you left.

Imagine you could get on a rocket and go to outer space and visit another planet where everything is perfect. Eventually, you must come back to earth, and when you get here, it's a little worse than when you left because things got neglected when you went away. Feeling the increased pressure from reality, you leave again. But each time you do, you come back, and it's worse than it was before. So, you must leave more often until eventually, you hit rock bottom. This is how it is with an escape of any kind. Sex is no different.

The thing about feeding your flesh is that the law of diminishing returns eventually kicks in. Let me explain; when you give your body something it wants that isn't the best thing for it, the next day it wants more of that thing. For example, if I eat one cookie one day the next day I want two. It was the same way for me with sex. As I fed that appetite, I had to have more to get the same enjoyment out of it. Afterward, it would leave me feeling empty. Not only did I have to do it again to feel good, but I would have to do more of it to get the same result. That's the way the spiral goes until you ride it all the way to the bottom. The Urban Dictionary uses porn to define diminishing returns, which is apropos here: "The more porn you watch, the more hardcore the porn has to be for you to get an erection and to finish."

I know most people won't live at this extreme. But this is where the road of sex without commitment can lead, even if we never get to the end of it. This is the road many are on, thinking, if only we had more then we'd be happy. Folks, it's not true, it's a dead end. Trust me I know.

A lot of the friends I used to party with who never got off that road of instant gratification aren't doing so good right now. The only answer is to realize that you are headed in the wrong direction and do an about-face. The Bible calls this repentance, but don't let the biblical word scare you. To repent is derived from the military phrase to "turn away." Imagine you are marching in one direction, you realized you're lost and headed down the wrong road, then you REPENT, do a 180 and begin marching in the other direction. This is what I did many years ago, and I've had to do many times since. My desire to march in in the right direction changed even if my actions didn't always line up. The good news is God is there the moment we repent and ask Him for help. He is waiting on you to simply choose His way for your life.

HELPMATE: GOD'S INTENTION FROM THE BEGINNING

If we take it back to where it all started, God made woman to be a "helpmate" to man. A companion, if you will, to come alongside and help him in his life and his work. Ladies don't shoot me. Remember, we as men are supposed to "love you as Christ loved the church." Also, Eve in and of herself is described in the Bible as "the glory of man" (I Cor. 11:7) She was sculpted to "make known the riches of God's glory upon vessels of mercy." (Rom. 9:23). Eve was God's creation, made for God's glory just as man was made for God's glory.

What's interesting here is Adam never said he needed or even FELT he needed a companion. Eve wasn't Adam's idea; he didn't create her.

We see that Adam was busy doing the work of God. It was GOD who saw it wasn't good for Adam to be alone. In His infinite intelligence, He knew Adam needed a helpmate. God knew him deeper than Adam knew himself. So, He created Eve to complete what He began when He created Adam. In other words, had God made Eve first he would have made Adam as well because they needed each other.

He charged them both to go forth and be fruitful and multiply (one of my favorite commands :). It wasn't until Eve came into the picture that Adam was able to work toward fulfilling that purpose and God-given assignment. We know that Adam and Eve forfeited the promise by disobeying God ... but does anyone ever wonder what life would be like today if they had been obedient? God didn't go back and give them sex organs *after* the fall; they were made to have sex at the beginning, before sin. The fall of man had nothing to do with sex. That belief is something that, unfortunately, the ancient church propagated, but it is not biblical. Sex existed in the garden when everything was still perfect. It just existed as God intended; it existed between Adam and Eve as husband and wife. How did Adam and Eve become husband and wife? Did they have a wedding? Did Eve wear a white dress? Did her father walk her down an aisle and give her away?

Eve's father, God, did give her to her husband Adam, but there was no wedding, no exchange of vows and rings in front of friends and family. Eve became Adam's wife when he had sex with her. That was the original act of marriage. When you fully grasp that truth it becomes incredibly clear exactly what the proper order for sex and marriage was always supposed to be.

I believe to have a successful life you need to have a successful rela-tionship. Once you realize your purpose in life and start going after it, you need to come home to a place where things are working and to someone who supports you. If you don't have that it will be much tougher if not impossible to reach your full potential. You may never accomplish your purpose in life without that cheerleader at home. That being said; the sex isn't the prize, the helpmate is! Stepping into your destiny and doing everything you were put on this earth to do while having a partner by your side to help you do it is the prize. Sex is the icing.

THE GREATER THE SACRIFICE THE GREATER THE REWARD

Because this road is difficult, it's important not to forget what we are vying for here. It is no small thing. It's the life that you've always wanted, and the person created for you to share it with. I think, too often, we forget how good the prize is at the end of the wait. I had a close, single friend who recently got engaged to the woman of his dreams after waiting five years tell me, "If I would have known how good it would be I, would have waited a lifetime." Now, of course, he wasn't saying that a year ago before he met her. He was bitching and moaning about how hard it was to be single and abstinent. But again, that's because he didn't realize how good it was going to be when it did happen. When I go to my morning boot camp class, and I suck wind for that forty-five minutes, first thing in the morning, it's painful. It's always after that strenuous workout that the benefit comes, and I'm never sorry that I went.

I competed in a few bodybuilding shows when I was younger. The preparation to get your body in that kind of condition is grueling. Waking up to do forty-five minutes of intense cardio at the crack of dawn (sometimes before bed too), rigorous resistance training, a super strict diet that consists of things like egg whites, broccoli, chicken breast, sweet potatoes, and not much else, is not fun. But, after about twelve weeks of following this, a body makes some incredible changes, and you're typically ready to step on stage.

It didn't take much to distinguish between the people who put in the work and those who didn't. I never wanted to be the fat guy on stage posing in my underwear; therefore, I did what it took to get the desired results. And why did I make all these sacrifices? For a trophy. Something I would throw in my closet to collect dust and all but forget about one day. My body would return to its previous condition in a surprisingly short amount of time, and that would be that. I don't know about you, but it only takes me about two weeks of cheating on my diet, and I can blow three months of work.

It's funny how people will gladly get up early to go to the gym, lift weights, do cardio, eat bland food, and deprive themselves for something that is temporary. Why do we find it so easy to make sacrifices for things so temporary, but struggle to make the same level of sacrifice when it comes to finding a partner for life?

But what is the prize for doing the hard work when it comes to dating and refraining from sex? A soulmate and the life we all yearn for. That is a prize worth working for. Is any of this so surprising though? Would you see someone who was lean and muscular, with six-pack abs and a cable vein shooting down their arm and not assume they worked for it? Of course not. We all know you don't get a body like that unless you make some temporary sacrifices and put your time in. The same is true if we want to have a great relationship and find true love. We must do the work.

The Bible says, "no discipline feels pleasant at the time but painful, later on however it yields a harvest of righteousness and peace for those who are trained by it." Be willing to "go through" it. No one gets to their promised land without going through some wilderness. The wilderness is uncomfortable; it's unfamiliar, sometimes it's flat-out painful. But know there is something great on the other side for you if you make the journey.

Waiting is worth it. I know it's hard. I know first-hand the difficulty of being the lone single in a world of couples. Society is built around couples and families, and that is a good thing. Don't allow yourself to fall into the trap of feeling you have to have a partner. It takes time and effort to be good at being alone, but it can be done.

One of the ways to manage is to seek out close relationships with family and deep non-romantic relationships with people of both genders, which I will get into in a later chapter. I can honestly say that I directly attribute much of my success in waiting this long, to having close platonic friends, which in many ways has been the biggest blessing of my life.

DON'T TRADE INTIMACY FOR SEX

Often, we don't learn to manage our sexual appetite. As a result, people trade an intimate relationship for a physical one with the wrong partner and wind up less happy than they were when they weren't having sex. I see this happen a lot amongst my friends. In the book, *I Kissed Dating Goodbye*, author Joshua Harris, states that "The joy of intimacy is the reward of commitment." He goes on to write that "All of us want intimacy. It means being close to someone. It's giving to and receiving from another person the deepest part of who we are—our hopes, our fears, our secrets, our affections. An intimate relationship in which we know and are known by another human is one of the most fulfilling and precious parts of life—it's a gift from God." I know from personal experience that the time in my life when I was having sex with the most women, I felt the most depressed and empty. I attribute that to the fact that sex does not equate to intimacy. Sex with someone you don't love, while it can be enjoyable and fun at the moment, leaves you feeling empty and unfulfilled because what we desire even more than sex is to be known.

Making love is a term that gets thrown into the mix with all the other expressions for having sex, which I don't need to repeat here; you know them all. However, that one term is different from all the others because it is unique. It is what marital sex is supposed to be, and at our core, it is what we are looking for when we hook up with a stranger or keep going back to that guy or gal who has broken our heart in the past. We are looking for a love that transcends. For one person who knows us completely and yet loves us unconditionally. That is why I believe God gave us marriage and sex. He knew what we needed most because He created us. He is the inventor and designer of everything, so He knows best how it all works. God gave us sex as a way to connect with another human being in a way we don't with any other and to connect with only one other human being. So that in that connection we experience that deep need to be known and loved.

Our search for this kind of love culminates in marriage, and that is where our pre-marital activities cause us trouble. This is a tragedy because marriage is not only the pinnacle of our romantic relationship and the foundation of the family it is also the bedrock of our society.

In "Soul Cravings," Erwin Raphael McManus writes, "Sex can be the most intimate and beautiful expression of love. We are only lying to ourselves when we act as if sex is proof of love. Too many men demand sex as proof of love. Too many women have given sex in hopes of love. We live in a world of users where we abuse each other to dull the pain of loneliness. We all long for intimacy, and physical contact can appear as intimacy, at least for a moment." Sex is a part of an intimate expression; sex is not intimacy.

Real intimacy is not found just by merging bodies in sex. When God said in Genesis 2:24, "and the two shall become one ..." He meant more than just the physical. After all, how many couples hop in bed together, share their bodies, but not their hearts? Undoubtedly, many of these people would say they are very lonely. Just as a garden hose is not the source of water, but only one expression, or vehicle for it, sex is not the source of intimacy, but an outlet or expression of it. No matter how hard you try, if real emotional and spiritual intimacy does not exist before sex, it is either impossible or incredibly difficult after.

* * * * * *

Waiting for Mr. or Mrs. Right may be difficult and will require you to learn to live inside this beautiful tension. But it all starts with managing that natural appetite for sex and a partner so you're not choosing the first Tom, Dick, or Harry or Tina, Danielle, or Henrietta that shows you attention. As I said, I see this happen a lot amongst my friends. Someone will be in the group enjoying all the friendships they are making and life in general. Then they start dating and hop in the sack with the first person that comes along and start focusing all their attention on the new person. This causes them to pay less attention to and lose those special, intimate friendships they've developed. Because their priorities are out of order, they wind up with neither intimacy nor friendship. Again, when you don't have intimacy with your partner, eventually physical attraction fades and the desire to have sex with them fades (or their desire to have sex with you fades.)

So how do we do it? We learn to manage our God-given appetite for sex and a companion. We decide in our heart of hearts to wait to marry to have sex. Not because it's a commandment or it's a sin to have sex, but because we want to achieve long-term happiness! It's a selfish move when you think about it. The way God designed it is a perfect balance.

As bad as I want to have sex again, I equally don't want to go through the pain of a divorce. I believe if I wait and choose carefully, I will avoid ending up with the wrong person; saving myself pain and heartache, which increases my odds of meeting the right person by remaining available when they do come along. One day, I believe, a woman will come along who I will be willing to pay the price for and with whom I will want to spend the rest of my life. I won't need to "sample the merchandise" beforehand because I will be in love with the person she is.

GOOD INTENTIONS AREN'T ENOUGH

Good intentions aren't enough. If you commit to doing this, it is going to cost you. If you are serious about having all the things you want most in life, and everything that God has for you, there are certain sacrifices you will need to make to put yourself in a position to succeed. It was not comfortable and simple for me, and it won't be for you. There will be a struggle, there will be lonely times, there will be hardship, you may be depressed at times, it can be an emotional roller coaster; but on the other side of it, there's this victory, there is a beautiful freedom that comes with it.

In my case, it wasn't an easy thing to do when you come from a past like mine. I didn't go from having sex with hundreds of women to none, without a struggle. Whatever part of me that was missing or broken that made me feel I needed to validate myself in that way didn't just go away. It was my identity. If I wasn't the Rob who was good at picking up girls, who was I? That took some time to figure out. When I first started this journey, I felt incomplete without a girlfriend. For my whole adult life, I had always had a girl beside me. I had fed my sexual animal so much it was stronger than my willpower. Even though I managed to be abstinent for long periods of time, I still wrestled with memories from my past and struggled with pornography. But when God gave me a vision I didn't want to disappoint Him. He believed in me so who was I not to believe in myself? But along with the belief He had in me came expectations and responsibility. Therefore, I made changes. In the beginning, I had to "white knuckle" it for a while. My emotions would swing from feeling lonely to horny; often, I felt depressed and wanted to feel something, anything. It's what I imagine going through withdrawal to a substance is like. I still to this day go home frustrated some nights because the desire for a woman is strong. At times I feel lonely and crave affection. I love women just as much now as I did back then. But my priorities have changed; my reverence and respect for women have changed. Trust me when I say it was not easy.

Hiring a life coach was a tremendous help for me. Life Coaching helped me find focus and my purpose. It also helped me set strong boundaries. As a result, today, I am surrounded by gorgeous women, with beautiful hearts on a daily basis. Instead of jeopardizing those relationships for twenty minutes of fun, I covet them. It feels so much better to be viewed as a man of substance, who can be trusted, whom people can confide in, and depend on. Trust me; I wasn't always the man I am today. Not to say I'm perfect. I still have thoughts and desires to do the wrong thing A LOT. The difference now, I don't act on them. I think most people think that when they change those desires go away, or if they do have a desire then they have to act on it like there's no choice involved. It doesn't work like that. Temptation or the DESIRE to do the wrong thing isn't sinful; it's when we act on those desires that we wind up suffering. I can want to eat pizza every day, but if I never actually do it and continue to eat salads, then guess what, I don't get the empty calories. Now I will say the longer you're on this path, the less the desires for the wrong things get, but I don't believe it ever completely goes away. Not in this life at least. The main thing is to not get discouraged with yourself and focus on progress not, perfection. God doesn't expect these deep-seated needs to disappear right away.

CHAPTER TEN
SET YOURSELF UP
FOR SUCCESS

"I hated every minute of training, but I said, 'Don't quit.
Suffer now and live the rest of your life as a champion.'"
Muhammad Ali

Hopefully by now maybe you're starting to see the value in waiting and thinking I might be right. So, the next topic I'd like to cover is HOW to wait. Because agreeing that something is right and doing it are two different things.

So how do we set ourselves up for success, should we choose to wait? Well, the first thing is setting some clear-cut boundaries up front. Everyone needs to establish his or her personal boundaries. You must know yourself and be honest with yourself about what you can and can't do when it comes to dating. For some people, their boundary may not be spending time alone together. Others may not be able to even kiss or hold hands. The main thing is to "know thyself." Don't try to see how close you can get to the fire without getting burned. Like guardrails on the side of the road, your boundaries should be something you try to steer clear of, not things you see how close you can get to without hitting.

To decide where your boundaries are you must be very honest with yourself about what you can handle. Many of us want to pretend we can do more than we can because it's fun to "play" with fire. Too often, we get burned, and the consequences are the same as if we hadn't tried at all. Know your triggers. Know what causes you to go down a path that would lead you to fail. Then set your boundaries up BEFORE you get to that place and communicate them to your new prospective partner right away. Decide where your line is before ever putting yourself in a compromising situation, so you don't make a mistake. Trying to decide where your boundaries are when you're already horizontal is a bad idea. This way when (notice I didn't say "if") you do fall into temptation, there is still a ledge there to fall onto, so you don't go over the cliff. DO NOT skate the line or you are setting yourself up for failure.

Even my friends who don't believe Jesus was the Son of God will say, at the very least, he was the most enlightened person to walk the earth, and what did Jesus say about sin? He said, "If your eye causes you to sin to gouge it out." Think about that. Can you imagine gouging out your own eye? Friends ask if it's ok to cuddle or spend the night at each other's house while they are dating. While there may not be anything technically wrong with cuddling, per se, I would ask "Is it worth it?" Not cuddling may sound extreme to some, but it's not as extreme as gouging out your own eye! My girlfriends miss this aspect of a relation-ship. While cuddling may be innocent to them, it's not always innocent to the guy. As an example, imagine a couple plans to chill around the house and watch a movie. They've also decided to wait to have sex. They agree to spend a cold, rainy day snuggled up together on the couch binge-watching the latest popular series on TV, and nothing happens.

The night went well, they kept their promise. They may have kissed a little. But they both maintained their boundaries. A couple weeks go by and because that previous Netflix-chill-session went well, they decide to do it again. This time, kissing leads to a heavy make-out session and before you know it, they have sex. Their intentions were admirable. But those are the consequences when we don't uphold strong boundaries. What started out as an innocent date, spun out of control and lead to a decision they both regretted. I think we must treat sin as serious as Jesus did. Treat sin like it's AIDS. You don't play with AIDS. You keep it far away from you. Do the same with sin, especially sexual sin. The Bible explicitly warns us, "Flee fornication." (I Corinthians 6:18) It tells us to run away. Why? Because nothing has the potential to wreck our lives as much as sex does. Famous Pastor Andy Stanley told his congregation once that he knows when someone comes to him for counseling and leads off with "I've never told anyone this," or "I've held this secret for years," that he is about to hear something about a sexual sin. I'm paraphrasing him, but his point in that sermon was that nothing wounds as deeply as sex, nothing is as personal, nothing has the potential to wreck our lives like sex. We carry that damage around with us and take it into our relationships. As I said before, I'm not religious. I get flak from church people sometimes for cussing, I don't have a problem with it or see whom it's hurting. Sex on the other hand? That is something different altogether. That same verse about fleeing continues and says, "All other sins a person commits outside the body, but the person that sins sexually sins against their own body." It puts sexual sin in a category of its own. If the consequences weren't severe, God wouldn't tell us to run from it. Where else in the Bible does God tell His people to literally run away?! When you become comfortable with temptation, you should run.

Men, this is where your leadership must come in, and where you need to speak up. Women can sit close and cuddle under a blanket and be perfectly happy with just that, while most men will become aroused. Even though women understand how a man works, they often don't think about it. When she suggests you come over to her place to hang out alone be straight with her that there have to be some hard, fast ground rules and either stick to them or don't hang out alone.

Spooning leads to forking. We need to be realistic and smart here. When a woman says "I just wanted to be held" she is likely telling you the truth. But all that matters is what you can handle at that moment. I'll say it again, intentions count for nothing. I can say "I meant to go to the gym today," but how many calories did I burn by staying home? You guessed it, none. I have not dated for any length of time on this path of waiting until marriage so I can't speak to how hard that must be. I can imagine when I do and start moving towards marriage it will be extremely difficult to wait. I've had several conversations with friends who waited, and they gladly share the boundaries they established to maintain their convictions, like "don't touch anywhere that is covered in clothes. Go home before 11:00 pm, so you don't fall asleep or start making out. Avoid sleeping in the same bed together. Refrain from conversations about future sex acts with each other. Have an accountability partner."

The key to not falling into temptation where sex is concerned is ensuring the other person has the same goals and values. If your views differ on this matter, one person will never be strong enough to hold out on their own. If you are a good man, and she is a good woman, and the attraction is mutual, as you date your connection and desire for one another will increase. It is in those moments that it's crucial to be of like mind. When one person is struggling with their desire for their mate, the other will need to prop the other up in that moment of weakness.

To make it to your wedding night without having sex is going to be very difficult. It's not going to happen by accident. It's going to take a hell of a lot of work. It would be the equivalent to running a marathon, and no one runs a marathon by accident. You must prepare for it. It takes a lot of discipline. You are not going to make it to your wedding night unless you're very disciplined. The great news … it can be done, and the reward at the end will be worth it! Boundaries are a must.

MY PERSONAL BOUNDARIES

To accomplish my goals, I had to make sweeping changes. I cut everyone off and changed everything about my life. I gave up the people I hung out with, the places I went, and the things I spent my time doing. People say they want to make changes but continue doing the same stuff, hanging out with the same people, and going to the same places.

Yet, they expect change. Sometimes they even use excuses like, "I want to be a good friend" or "I want to help them." It's like being on the airplane when those masks come down; first, you must put the mask on yourself before trying to help the person next to you. You can't help someone else if you can't breathe.

Trying to make changes while continuing to do the same things as before *is like crabs* trying to crawl out of *a bucket.* Each person holds the other down, keeping the other person stuck inadvertently, and no one ever gets out. First, you must step away from everyone. Get yourself healthy. Then go back, one by one, and pull people up. That is the only way. Even still, this can be dangerous.

Let me give an example. A few years ago, I reconnected with a girl from my past. I'd known her for the better part of fifteen years. She was going through a divorce and began attending my church. I befriended her and pulled her close to my group of friends. I could immediately see her making better decisions as the group positively influenced her.

She and I had a certain level of comfort because we had known each other so long, having come from similar backgrounds. We began spending more time together. She was attractive, but I was determined to remain friends with her because I was looking for something more than just physical attraction. I had been praying about whom to date next and was waiting for God to give me the green light on someone. God hadn't said anything about this girl. But I was enjoying my time with her, and we continued to grow closer.

We had never been physical in any way. We had never even held hands. We flirted quite a bit and used pet names for each other. I could feel us getting closer and the situation becoming dangerous. When I brought it up to her, saying, the potential to make a mistake was there she thought it was stupid that I wanted to back away and spend less time together. She made me feel as if us getting physical could never happen. "We're too good of friends, I would never allow that," she swore. Although I knew in the back of my mind that wasn't true, I let her convince me.

The next time that we spent time together we had sex. It was a huge blow at the time. I had been abstinent for three years and believed that I was stronger than that. But once we started kissing, I couldn't pull the emergency brake to stop it. Things spiraled out of control quickly, and it almost ended our friendship.

That experience led to the personal boundaries I have now. For the last three years, I decided not to spend time alone with women because I know myself. I know that it is dangerous for me, given my past and my weaknesses in that area. I might ride in a car or go to the movies with a woman. But, I wouldn't have a girl at my house alone to watch a movie or vice versa.

The last time I hung out with a girl at my house, we watched a movie and wound up hooking up. I will not run that risk again. I keep these limits for SELFISH REASONS. I don't want to burn a friendship, hurt another person, damage the faith that other people have placed in me and lose credibility, get stuck with the wrong person, get an STD, or get someone pregnant. Does that make sense? But hey, those are my boundaries, and I admit they may seem extreme. I implore you to be selfish in this area and set strong boundaries as well.

I removed all obstacles from my life that would prevent me from succeeding. In addition to not spending time alone with women, I quit drinking and have been sober now for over six years because I liked to have sex when I drank. I can't tell you how much more productive this one decision has made me, and it all stemmed from my desire to wait to have sex until marriage.

I will add that the question regarding alcohol has come up before, "Will you ever drink again one day?" Who knows, maybe when I'm married I'll be able to drink in moderation. All I do know is it wasn't working for me, so I decided to put it down. I think too many people get hung up on quitting because they feel, to do so, they must admit they are an "alcoholic" and commit to never drinking again. That may very well be the case. Who am I to say? But I think it's ok to say, "This isn't working for me at this point in my life." You may decide to take six months (or whatever amount of time) off and reevaluate it after some time and see what your life is like at that point. I know I've had more than a few friends do it this way and found that life is better without alcohol, so they want to keep it going. I don't think, "I can't drink ever again," I think, "I don't want it because life is good without it." But, again, that's just me.

I recommend setting boundaries before you ever go on the next date. I want to offer some suggestions on how to safeguard your relationship while spending quality time with your significant other. So here are some boundaries I would suggest. Below are some I believe are sound, that I will pass along to you:

Be upfront about your boundaries in romantic situations

Go out together with friends

Get to know each other in group settings and see how the other person relates to people

Avoid being together in private, e.g., car, room, other quiet places. (Catch public transport instead of driving. Chat with each other in the middle of a fast food restaurant, instead of in your home/room.)

Stay away from graphic depictions of sex.

Tell your friends about your decision to wait (ACCOUNTABILITY)

Remain firm in your beliefs even if it means leaving events or parties, cutting off people, sacrifices, etc.

Make sure you are working together to wait!

SEX TRANSMUTATION

In the bestselling book and "Granddaddy of all motivational literature," *Think and Grow Rich*, author Napoleon Hill, points out that, "Sexual desire is the strongest of all human desires." Hill writes that it is a well-known fact that many great people throughout history, including inventors, leaders, and people of notable achievement across all spectrums used their sex drive as fuel." He calls this *Sex Transmutation*. The word transmute means "the transferring of one form of energy into another." Sex transmutation is quite literally just channeling sexual energy from purely physical expression to some other nature.

Hill goes on to write that sex has three functions: 1) Reproduction 2) Therapeutic 3) The transformation of mediocrity to genius through transmutation. Did you catch that last one? According to Hill sexual desire is a powerful energy that when redirected can produce amazing results including "keenness of imagination, courage, will-power, persistence, and creative ability." Hill goes on to rightly state that "so strong and impelling, is the desire for sexual contact that men freely run the risk of life and reputation to indulge it. (But) when harnessed, and redirected along other lines, this motivating force maintains all its attributes which may be used as powerful creative forces in any profession or calling, including, of course, the accumulation of riches." When you focus all your energy on winning the affections of another person your mind fires on all cylinders, the same thing happens when you put all that passion into a business or idea that you may have.

Speaking from experience, no truer words have ever been spoken (in this case written). Taking the time to work on myself and getting to know myself as a sober, single man was one of the best decisions I ever made. Over the last six-plus years, I've redirected all the energy I previously used chasing the opposite sex and have instead used it for other purposes. I used my "time off" to start a nonprofit I'm deeply passionate about, cultivate an amazing group of friends, read more than I ever have before, go on several relief trips to third world countries, become a leader at my church, and become very involved in serving my community. I rechanneled all that sexual energy to do the hard work on myself to have the life that I wanted.

The unexpected benefit of waiting to have sex was filling my time with good things that made me a better person. Instead of going to bars at night and tying one on, I went to bed and got up early, read or worked out. I spent quiet time talking to God or meditating to get a clear picture of my purpose in life. All the extra hours without a foggy brain from a late night of consuming alcoholic beverages proved to be very beneficial in helping me move the needle forward in the areas of my life that mattered most.

By spending more time with my family, being a better friend, getting my exercise routine on point, working with a life coach, setting goals, working my ass off, consuming books at a feverish pace, and getting my diet down to a science, I became the best version of myself. All because I decided to wait to have sex until marriage. I took all that energy and redirected into bettering myself instead of looking for another person. In doing so, I believe I did what was necessary to attract the person who I can be happy with for the long term. So many people want to skip this part and get to that other person who will "complete them." But in my experience, it rarely, if ever happens like that. Stop trying to skip the struggle. Struggle builds character.

All this was a direct benefit of choosing to wait. I'm at a place now in my life where I'm living a more fulfilled life than ever before. I wake up early every morning excited to tackle the day and leave my mark on the world. Before when I was drinking, the mornings were the hardest time of day for me because I would wake up and not like the reality I had created for myself. Was I having sex? Yes. Was I happy? No. Deciding to wait has affected every other area of my life and enabled me to get to the place I wanted to be most. However, I had to sacrifice many of the things that I wanted at the moment. I still do. I share that because I know what I'm proposing to you is possible; I did it.

Being single is an incredible opportunity if you use it right. When you learn to manage that sexual appetite, you can take all that time and energy you would've directed toward selfish pursuits that led nowhere and helped no one and direct it toward helping others! I'll say it again, waiting to have sex has proven to be the most beneficial thing I have ever done. The energy I once poured into attracting the opposite sex is now spent running my organization, improving my mind, cementing my relationship with God, and building my friendships.

ONE YEAR CHALLENGE

Hollywood has given us a distorted view of love and convinced us that when we find the "right person," they will complete us, and we will live happily ever after. In my humble, but accurate opinion, I believe this is a lie and sets us up for trouble in dating and marriage.

Andy Stanley has a series entitled the "New Rules, for Love, Sex and Dating." The message is about *becoming* the right person rather than *looking for* the right person. He follows it up with an idea he called the "One Year Challenge." He dares singles who were actively dating and making selfish decisions, to take a one-year sabbatical from dating, flirting, texting (sexting), etc., and focus that time, instead, on themselves.

The idea was to be intentional about eliminating dating and use that energy instead to focus on self-improvement. During that time people could learn to love themselves, love God and eventually learn to start dating the way God intended. The primary focus of the challenge was to learn what kind of person you want, then spend your time *becoming* the person someone of quality would want to date and marry. Ultimately, "We do not attract what we want, but what we are," says James Allen, author of "As a Man Thinketh." So how do we become the right person?

The One-year challenge is straightforward. If you are having a hard time finding a date or coming out of a bad relationship, pump the brakes and take time to work on YOU. Get finances, personal habits, work habits in order, so that when you do begin a relationship, you can start from a position of strength. I have several girlfriends who have taken this challenge, and I've seen it produce tremendous results in their lives. One of the main benefits of taking time off to focus on yourself is that it teaches you how not to be love "thirsty." You learn to be happy alone, and when you aren't dependent on another person to make you happy, you can wait for someone whom you want versus choosing someone out of desperation. It may sound silly, but a good piece of advice someone gave me once was "never grocery shop while you're hungry." Why? Because you always take home something that you'll regret later. That is what dating out of loneliness is like. Always remember, it's better to be single and lonely than with the wrong person and unhappy.

SIX MONTH CHALLENGE

Instead of a one-year challenge … I challenge you to commit to six months of abstinence. It can improve your life exponentially. If you decide to take this challenge, there are ways to set yourself up for success. The first thing I believe you need to do is find a friend to share your commitment with who will support your decision. I don't mean your bar-hopping friend who will ask you why in the hell would you do that. You want a friend who will understand and be your accountability partner. Hopefully, they will even do it with you if they haven't already done it themselves.

For me, that person was Billy Loften. We worked out together. We hung out on the weekends, went to the movies, and went out to eat, all while sharing the challenges we faced. This sharing mostly consisted of us bitching about how hard it was to remain abstinent and questioning whether it was even worth it.

I could not have made it this far without a wingman like Billy. I would have given up long ago. Even with a solid wingman, it was probably the hardest thing I've ever done, he would say the same. But remember the story about my friend who said he would have waited a lifetime? It was Billy. He met and fell in love with a beautiful woman named Ariana at a game night at his house a couple years ago. The girl immediately caught his eye, but Billy just kind of watched her from a distance. He noticed how she handled herself in different situations and got to know the woman she is. His interest grew, and eventually, he shared his feelings with her. The funny thing was, she didn't reciprocate his feelings initially.

However, Billy couldn't shake the feeling in his bones that she was the one for him. The Bible says, "Love is patient," (I Corinthians 13: 4) so Billy continued to wait patiently for her. He remained friends with her while praying and asking God for His plan. Two years after meeting the girl, her heart changed. She began to see Billy. I don't mean date him, I mean, something changed in her heart, and she was able to *see* him. He had been there all along, but she started seeing him in a different light and saw all the good qualities about him. I'm happy to say they will be married later this year.

It was through their friendship that the romance developed. I can't promise it will always work out this way, but I think that is an excellent example of how two people of the opposite sex can be just friends, even if there is some level of attraction on the part of one person.

HUSTLE WHILE YOU WAIT

In his book "I Kissed Dating Goodbye" Joshua Harris writes that one of his mom's favorite quotes was *hustle while you wait*. To, as he puts it, "be productive during a lull in the action." Don't just sit around for six months not doing anything waiting for someone to come along and sweep you off your feet, but use your time off as a single person productively. Make the most of the opportunity. Develop your skills, start a business, volunteer, go back to school, make great friends. These will all be valuable assets to take into marriage and help you to better attract a higher quality mate or that "right person."

Plus, if you don't do these things when your single do you honestly think it will be easier to do them when you are in a relationship and have someone else's happiness to worry about? Remember we attract what we are not what we want. Many people stunt their growth because they jump into a romantic relationship prematurely before they have developed. Like a baby takes nine months in the womb to completely develop, there are certain ways we mature that can only happen when we stop using a relationship as a crutch, expecting it to "complete us." Take the time to make the most of being single and prepare yourself for the next season of life.

It's unrealistic to think that when we get married everything will change. Become the best version of you; then you will attract the best possible mate. Jesus said, "if you are faithful with a few things you will be faithful with much." Be faithful with what you have right now and then you will be better prepared to handle the much when you do get into a relationship.

PURPOSE

Some of my friends who know I've been abstaining from sex and waiting for Mrs. Right say things like "What if there isn't a payoff?" They are asking, "What if you never find love and meet your soulmate?" I always say the same thing, "There already has been a payoff. I've discovered my purpose." Not counting the work I've done in the community, both personally and through the church, the places I've traveled, all the amazing friendships I've developed, the lives God has allowed me to impact, and I am in the process of opening a bar (HOME) that will change the social landscape of the city I live in and, I believe, many other cities. What is that worth? I'd venture to guess a lot of people never find their purpose. I found mine by giving up a few years of meaningless sex with people whose names I wouldn't remember now and using that energy to put into things that last. I'd say that was a damn good trade. I've gotten my reward already. Finding love will be the cherry on the sundae.

There's a verse in the Bible that says, "**Do not conform** to the pattern of this **world** but be transformed by the renewing of your mind. Then you will be able to test and approve what God's will is – His good, pleasing and perfect will." (Romans 12:2)

This was one of the first verses I memorized when I decided to follow Jesus.

The first half of the verse means that we shouldn't copy the way everyone around us acts, but instead, we should be different, set apart. When our behavior changes we start to think differently. The second half of the verse, and this is the part that gets less attention, says that after we do this THEN we will be able to "test and approve what God's will is." I know a lot of people who want to know their purpose yet struggle to find it. This verse tells us that if we start living right that He will show it to us. I don't know if you've ever walked with God, but I can tell you that there's nothing like being in the center of God's will for your life. You could have all the material possessions, the perfect job, and that right person on paper, but if you are outside of the will of God for your life, it won't give you that deep fulfillment that all of us want.

There is a direct correlation between our behavior (obedience) and finding our purpose and a sense of deep fulfillment. When you are living outside the will of God life is meaningless and difficult. Not to say, it's always roses and sunshine inside the will of God, but you know there's a purpose in the pain and that you are living for something bigger than your selfish desires. There is peace inside God's will. Outside the will of God, you have a nagging feeling you know you were created to do something more.

I believe much of this is directly related to the fact that we are living in a way that makes it hard, if not impossible, to hear God's voice in our life. We hang onto things and people, that were we to let go, God could speak to us, and we would hear Him. Remember, Adam and Eve's life got hard AFTER they sinned. Up until then, life was good and easy. They lived in paradise! But after they sinned God said, "By the sweat of your brow will you eat your food." The first time we see Man doing a job that required hard work is after sin entered the world, and it is still true today. I bring all this up because when I was living only for myself, and separated from God, I was having sex. It was enjoyable while I did it, but I was struggling and unfulfilled. Now, I'm not having any sex but feel deeply fulfilled in my life. I wake up excited to get to work and start my day because I absolutely love what I do. I feel like I'm living "HIS GOOD, PLEASING and PERFECT will." It comes at a price; the price is obedience. But the cost is pennies compared to the reward of having a relationship with Jesus.

There is something about human nature that makes us all want to be the kings and queens of our world. But, God set this whole thing up so that He is the only, true King. When we honor Him first and obey His commandments, He makes sure our needs are met and blesses us in a way we would never have imagined. Matthew 6:32 counsels us not to worry about what we're going to eat and wear and tells us that … "our Heavenly Father knows what we need." Then Matthew 6:33 gives us the promise that if we "seek first the kingdom of God and his righteousness that all these things will be added to you." In other words, if we seek righteousness and work to build up the kingdom of God, He will take care of our kingdom.

CHAPTER ELEVEN
FRIENDS WITH BETTER BENEFITS

"Call it a clan, call it a network, call it a tribe,
call it a family: Whatever you call it, whoever you are,
you need one."
Jane Howard

Around the end of 2011, my nightclub promotion career was coming to an end. I was still hanging on and scratching out a living, but I was miserable doing it. The love I had for it had left, and I was stuck doing something I hated with little to put on a resume if I did decide to venture out to find a "legit" job. One of my last parties was at a place in Baltimore called Red Maple. It was a nice little lounge where people could get tapas and dance. Because the place was a staple in the Baltimore nightlife, it didn't take a lot of work to fill it up, even though I didn't have the pull I'd once had. But I can remember the distinct feeling of being in a bar full of people and not knowing anyone there. I mean, I was the promoter. I was the guy. I remember looking around and not having any friends there. I mean there may have been some people there who knew my name, but no one that I could say cared about me or that I cared about. It was a depressing realization.

One of the saddest things is to be surrounded by people but feel alone. To be honest, I didn't have anyone to blame but myself; years of reckless living had sown a harvest in my life, and I was not enjoying the fruit. In 2006, when I had started promoting again, I had a great group of friends. We went out together, volunteered together, did life together. But my lack of self-control and self-discipline had led me to a place I did not enjoy.

I knew what I needed to do. I was the one who got myself into it, and I was the one to get myself out. It wasn't long after that night that I made the decision to rededicate myself to God and living a more disciplined life; things began to improve. I made genuine friends, and they were stronger than before. Why? Because great relationships are built on one thing, putting other people before yourself. This is what creates genuine community.

Real community comes when we add value to other people's lives. Sacrifice is what produces great relationships. If anyone has ever loved you unconditionally and gone out of their way for you, you know the kind of bond that forms. Have you ever had someone sacrifice for you and put your needs above their own? Didn't that produce a strong feeling of love for them? There are people in my life who have sacrificed for me that I would do anything for, including taking a bullet. Why? Because they sacrificed for me.

How many of you have a close friend? I don't mean someone you go drinking with on the weekends but someone who will help you move. How many of you have a friend you can call when you need help? When you need a shoulder to cry on? When you need to be comforted? When you need to vent? Someone you can share the deepest parts of your life with and know they will be discreet with what you shared? If you were asked what it was that keeps you happy and healthy as you go through life, what would you say? If you're like some people, you might answer that question by saying money or fame.

A lack of close friends, not Facebook Friends, but *close* friends, correlates with increased levels of depression and increased levels of stress. Humans are pack animals. We are designed to connect. We *need* other people in our lives for our emotional well-being. When you have fewer people to reach out to for emotional support when things go wrong, fewer people will have your back in a crisis. When we don't have a healthy emotional support system, we get stressed. We feel empty. Those feelings of isolation and helplessness contribute to a depressed immune system. Moreover, people who have fewer friends have higher levels of the stress hormone cortisol and greater cardiovascular issues. Studies show people with fewer friends tend to die sooner after having a heart attack than people with a dependable social network. Having a lot of close friends may even reduce your chance of catching a cold! Tasha R. Howe, Ph.D., Associate Professor of Psychology at Humboldt State University, states, "We are social animals, and we have evolved to be in groups. We have always needed others for our survival. It's in our genes."

People with a healthy social support system and close ties to friends and family have higher levels of emotional and material support when things go wrong. Again, this shouldn't be surprising. Our friends, after all, tend to rally to our side in times of crisis. People with more extensive social circles and more close friends also tend to have higher levels of self-esteem, which in turn gives them a greater feeling of control in their life. That feeling of security causes people to take better care of their health versus those who feel alone. When you have people you can turn to, you're more likely to seek out help when things are hard, and you don't feel like you can go on. People who have more friends also have lower blood pressure, lower levels of cholesterol, and an overall higher quality of life. In fact, people with more friends found their risk of death cut by *sixty percent* overall! Professor Howe said, "People with big social groups tend to be more at peace, which leads to better health."

An eighty-year-old Harvard study on adult life found that relationships and embracing community are what help us live happier, longer lives. This trait is common amongst us all. Even more than we want sex, we want intimacy with friends and with the person we choose as a partner.

During my nightclub promotion days, I put my needs and desires before the needs of those around me, especially the women I dated. After a while, I didn't have any women friends. I realized over time it's better to have long-term friends than short-term sex partners. Because I have found that life gets good when you have great relationships with others, that's what makes life rich. Therefore, we need people. You may disagree but stay with me here. In his popular book, "Where Good Ideas Come From," author Stephen Johnson puts forth the notion that most great ideas and inventions today come not from Brainiac scientists sitting alone in labs, but rather from collaborative environments. In addition, most people find jobs through other people, not by responding to classified ads. Pastor, author, and filmmaker, T.D. Jakes says "opportunities will come through relationships, people you value. There are some blessings that you cannot have without relationships. You cannot be fruitful by yourself." Therefore, it just makes sense to have as many great relationships as possible.

So why burn a relationship by having sex with someone that could be a great friend unless you're sure that that you want to go to that level with the person for the long term? If you do decide to get physical there's a very good chance someone will catch feelings and when that physical relationship ends you probably will lose that person as a friend.

How do you know the person you lost wasn't assigned by God to help you get your breakthrough? That person could be a missing piece in your puzzle or one to introduce you to the person who could help you become who you're ultimately meant to be. What if they hold one of the keys to your future? Some people will inevitably ask, "Can guys and women be just friends?" I believe that guys and girls can be great friends because I have some amazing platonic girlfriends. It's natural that in a group of a lot of singles that physical attraction forms between people, I mean come on, we are human! But the key here to not making it awkward is just don't be weird about it.

I have wonderful, women friends who have no romantic feelings for me and nor do I for them. We are more like brother and sister than anything.

Even though I'm not romantically attached to anyone right now, I have more girlfriends than I've ever had in my life. My relationships with women are the best they've ever been. I have some great, beautiful girl friends that I love doing life with. They add value to my life, and I believe I add value to theirs as well. One of the primary reasons I have such great friendships is because none of us have slept together. The moment that happens, everything changes. A friend asked me recently "How are you still single when you're surrounded by so many gorgeous and godly women? Surely, one of them would make a great wife." I agreed with her, almost all of the women I spend a good portion of my time around will make great wives to some very lucky men, but that doesn't mean that every girl I have common interests with that I'm attracted to, is for me. I think it's a good idea to wait and feel people out before asking someone on a date. Some people call this the friend zone. This will give you a chance to see that person in some different settings and how they react in each of them. It will also give you a chance to read your feelings to see if there's anything more because it's easy to be physically attracted to someone initially because of how God wired us.

This is where it gets a little more spiritual and a bit less practical, and if you're not a believer, you may have a hard time understanding or relating. I'll repeat, I'm not religious, but there is a point where you start to see the value in having a RELATIONSHIP with an all-knowing, all-loving, all-powerful God. God leads me, and gives me answers in various ways; surely, He is going to let me know who to date and marry. And trust me, we talk about this a lot. There have been more than a few girls in the group I thought I could've possibly seen something in, but God hasn't told me to move in this area, so I haven't. Plus, I've learned to be happy alone over the last several years, so while I do want a partner to share my life with, I'm not willing to settle and get ahead of God because I know how that ends. While I believe getting to know a woman before ever actually asking her out on a date is an excellent strategy to finding love, I'm also waiting on God to give me a clue on who and when I should date next. My Pastor's wife and life coach Lori Lockemy taught me a prayer that goes, "Do not arouse or awaken love until it so desires." Song of Songs 2:7 I believe if you have a relationship with God when the time comes He will make sure you don't miss it.

After attempting to walk this path of self-improvement alone for several years and failing miserably, I realized that to become the best version of yourself, we need community. I don't mean you need to live in a community. I mean you need genuine community. Speaking from personal experience, it doesn't matter how determined you are to be a better person; if you don't have good people around you to walk with you on your path to self-actualization you just won't make it, you cannot make it alone.

Becoming your best self will require you to make a series of right decisions over the long term and that just isn't possible to do by yourself. You will get discouraged and quit or get lonely or depressed and do something, whatever your thing is, that will take you out of the game. You need community to make it. There's an African Proverb that goes "If you want to go fast go alone, if you want to go far go together."

The funny thing is, when you decide to wait to have sex, you are FORCED to self-actualize in many ways because you don't have sex to fall back on. Not only are you forced to develop as a person on your own, to find yourself and what makes you happy; more importantly it forces you to cultivate great friendships. It's through these deep, meaningful, non-romantic intimate relationships that we find the love, support, and encouragement we need to become who we were meant to be. When you get serious about waiting you don't even have mindless dating to fall back on because you won't want to put yourself in a compromising situation unless you honestly believe it has a chance of going somewhere. By taking sex out of the equation, you open yourself up to more and richer relationships, therefore opening up the door to even more opportunities. Finally, it is my experience that none of that is possible without a personal relationship with Jesus. That fundamental connection to our creator helps us become a complete person and realize our full potential. I believe it's only when we do these things that we can be whole and who we need to be for someone else to have a successful relationship.

Over the last several years I've established great friendships because I had to. I had to develop these friendships to survive because once I committed to wait until marriage to have sex, I didn't have the luxury of just jumping from girl to girl anymore. Instead of filling the void with meaningless sex and short-term, doomed relationships, I cultivated a great group of friends and allowed Jesus to fill me, and as a result, I'm a better person, a better son and a better friend.

There is a direct link between your level of seriousness about waiting to have sex and your ability to connect to a healthy community. It's much like the language immersion technique. We'd all like to learn a foreign language and maybe even know we should, but it's usually only when we get dropped into a foreign country and have no choice but to learn it to survive that we ever do. If you have sex to fall back on or you are focused on finding your next sex partner, your need for real, genuine, healthy community decreases and so does your motivation to go out and find it. Ultimately this affects your ability to reach your full potential in life. We will never hit our full potential unless we learn to make, keep, grow, and cultivate real friends. We were made for deep, meaningful, friendships.

As a society, we have moved away from inter-dependence (or dependence on) God to independence and self-reliance. Therefore, some of us lead mediocre lives because we have forfeited the promise of fulfillment by settling and lowering our standards. We aren't allocating sufficient time and space for the person, who is meant to challenge, encourage, support, and uplift us ... to know us fully. Would the person who is created to walk this life with you even recognize you if you crossed paths? Are you so consumed with sex, heartache, anger, ego, and drama, ... that the person who holds a key to your purpose could walk past you without a glance because you aren't the man or woman they need you to be? Single men and women are doing great things, and many of them are highly successful. But what if greater lies in wait for you? What if that greater comes in the form of compassion, service, and overall added value to the world; the intangible things that cannot be measured by salary, homes or material means?

CITYFAM

A few years ago, my friend Billy Loften and I founded an organization that has become a movement with the potential to change the social landscape of every city in the world. It started out as just him and I, striving to make right decisions and become better versions of ourselves; but bored out of our minds having nothing fun to do on the weekends or people to do it with. It was 2012, I decided to quit promoting once and for all, and began the process of getting sober. But when the weekend came, there wasn't a whole lot to do. I wound up staying in and renting Redbox movies most nights by myself. After about a year of doing this, it got old. One day I was bitching to a friend, and he suggested I put some social outings together just to scratch the itch I had. He said something like, "you were a promoter, why don't you put together some events that won't cause you to F#*& Up?" I was still a little hesitant to give myself any amount of freedom, but I knew from past experiences that my strategy of sheltering myself from the world wasn't a long-term solution. Sooner or later I needed to have a social life, or I would just burn out like I did before. I started putting fun things together on the weekends for purely selfish reasons, pretty much anything to get myself out of the house. *Fun without regrets* as we like to call them now. They were lame at first, I'll admit. I would promote a movie night, and literally three people would show up ... and it was free! I even paid for the popcorn. Each event cost me money, but I figured it was an investment as I'd be spending money if I had gone out to a bar or something anyway. Plus, I knew the power in community. After several months of doing events, the group slowly began to grow. We went from four or five people showing up to a social event to thirty or forty.

On a personal level, I was getting more involved at a local faith community named Epic Church. Epic is very involved in the city I live in, so I began doing a good amount of giving back through them. The volunteering felt good, and I started liking myself again. God was using my service to others to heal me of my mess and my issues. I remembered that it had been years I wanted to give back and how long it took me to get started. I realized it was only through the church that I was able to get plugged in and thought surely there are people in our group that have a desire to serve and don't consider themselves "religious" or go to church. I wanted to give them an opportunity to volunteer, so they felt productive and useful too.

Billy and I started looking for worthwhile causes in the community for our group to get involved in between all of our social events. We grew even more. At that point, we realized this was something, and we had to give it a name, we called it CityFam. Many people want to give back and make a positive contribution, by helping the less fortunate, but often they don't know how to get started. At CityFam we remove the barriers to entry, by not only making it easy to get started but also making it fun.

I've found in general, most churches are filled with good people who genuinely want to help others and make a difference in people's lives. There's always some bad apples in the bunch, but we won't get into those because they are the minority and not representative of the churches I've attended. But the service-centered attitude I experienced when I gave my heart to Jesus and began to go to church was something new to me at the time. Coming from a world where everyone was looking out for number one, the people I met at church were a breath of fresh air. While I may have not been able to relate to them all that well, and even found some of the people strange, overall they were good people and genuinely looking out for each other's best interests. I noticed the attitude in Church was *what can I do for you?* The reverse was present in the bar scene; it was *what can I get from you?* So, one of the things we do at CityFam is breed a culture of sacrifice. We've taken the *what can I do for you* attitude and brought it into social settings. CityFam was born out of our desire to break free from the cycle of broken relationships and lives that had no purpose.

When people come to our events, they feel the difference. They always say the same thing, "Everyone's so nice!" And we're always like, "Yeah, they really are! And guess what? We're going to feed the homeless next week, would you like to come with us?" The response is always the same, "I've always wanted to do something like this, but I just didn't know how to get started." After they volunteer, they start feeling different about themselves. They begin to form healthy relationships. You see people make the most incredible changes. They become better versions of themselves because it's all about LOVE! And love = sacrifice. Cityfam envisions a community where all residents are "doing life" together by socializing, serving, and looking out for each other's best interest. We not only believe we can change our world; we can also impact positive change in one another. That is why one of the taglines we like to use at CityFam is "Friends with better benefits."

Over the past few years, CityFam has connected hundreds of people to serve at dozens of non-profit organizations. In addition, CityFam has organized and executed several International Relief Trips to serve the less fortunate in third world countries. There is nothing more motivating in life than finding a higher purpose and a community of people pulling for you to maximize your potential all while making the world around you better than you found it.

Now, finding other people like me completely consumes me. People staying at home, bored out of their minds on the weekend; or going out and making poor choices and thinking *what's the alternative?* The alternative is CityFam! Our organization is for anyone who wants to have fun but doesn't want to do anything they'll regret on Monday. It's for people who want to give back to their community but never knew how to get started. It's for anyone that wants to become the best version of themselves and have a supportive community of people to help them get there. We provide a judgment-free zone and meet people where they are. One of the first questions Billy and I asked ourselves when we first started it, was *why we were doing it*. We answered that question *because change happens through the context of relationships*. Authentic and supportive relationships create healthier communities. CityFam is a movement of like-minded people who want to enjoy life to the fullest. Don't worry if you're not a Baltimore resident; we plan to duplicate our efforts into other cities nationwide.

CityFam would have never come to fruition had I not given up sex. The lives I've seen transformed and improved through this organization would have never occurred in such a manner had I not given up sex. It cost me something. But that sacrifice led to greater things, greater purpose, greater passion, greater friendships, greater love. And through the sacrifice of abstinence, I have been able to live a more fulfilling and joyful life.

CLOSING

Hopefully, after reading this, you see why it makes sense to wait. The reason people don't want to wait isn't that they don't believe it's right, it's because it's hard. When you start feeling like giving up remember, EVERYTHING worth having is hard. Squats are hard. Dieting is hard. Getting an education is hard. Becoming successful is hard. Parenting is hard. Keeping your word is hard. By no means am I preaching to you here. The only reason I know the things I do is because I did EVERYTHING wrong! Some people learn from the mistakes of others, and some people must learn their lessons the hard way. I learned mine the hard way. My goal is to save you from some of the heartache I endured.

Here's the good news, regardless of where you are it's not too late! This plan works. I know from experience. *It's never too late to be who you might have been.* If you have a great relationship already, you might not need this, but you may know someone who does. If you are single and content with getting the same results everyone else is getting when it comes to love and happiness, then disregard everything you just read. Continue going about your dating and sex life the same as everyone else. BUT ... if you want more ... if you want meaningful, long-lasting relationships with close friends and a wonderful soulmate to share this life, then accept my six-month challenge and join the *Why Waiting Works Community* on Facebook for support and discussion. If you want something different, you must do something different. It will require embracing a revolutionary lifestyle. Keep your eyes on the prize and keep going. Take the energy and put it toward your dreams.

It won't be as brutal as my experience. You won't have to white knuckle it like I did, you won't be alone. We have a support system in place for you online and with CityFam. Meet new people, get connected, serve, and change your community, cultivate healthy relationships and have some fun. If the thought of inspiring and supportive friends who care about you and your well-being energizes you, then you have found your place.

Are you willing to break culture's rules to experience the best life has to offer you? One of my favorite quotes is, "Work while they sleep. Learn while they party. Save while they spend. Then live like they dream." You read that, and something jumps inside of you because you know it's true. What is the common thread in all those? Discipline and delayed gratification. It's the key to long-term happiness. I'd like to add one more to the list, "Wait while they won't, then love deeper than they ever will."

Do you "want to live like they dream?" Then be willing to do what they won't. That means waiting. Only three percent of the population waits. Will you be one of them, to have everything you've ever wanted in life? Are you ready to deny yourself what you want **right now**, to get what you want **most** in life?

What I've written here isn't a new concept, just a different perspective from what culture tells us to do today. Don't get to the end of your life and realize you traded real happiness for a few rolls in the hay. God forbid, you never find true love or love deeply because you linked up with someone going in the opposite direction of your dream and never accomplish your purpose; never hit your full potential … saying "How I hated discipline! How my heart spurned correction!" (Proverbs 5:12)

Remember, there are two types of pain in this world, the pain of discipline and the pain of regret. The pain of discipline is temporary but the pain of regret lasts forever. Choose wisely my friends.

If you enjoyed this book, please go and leave a review. It only takes a few minutes and reviews help other readers discover this book.

If you'd like to read this book again and talk it over with friends, the *Truth About Sex Small Group Study* makes this easy to do. This 8-week experience was designed for a group of people to gather around its potent content with a plan to socialize, connect and serve. If you'd like more information about starting a CityFam chapter in your part of the world or would like to be notified when we come to your area, visit WWW.CITYFAM.COM. To help me get this message out and earn rewards in the process become a member of my SUPERFAM! Go to WWW.ROBBKOWALSKI.COM and sign up today. You will be the first to get notified when I post new videos and promotions and I'll keep you updated on everything I'm working on.

As a thank you, subscribers get my *'Dating While Waiting Guide'* absolutely Free.

To book me for speaking engagements email BOOKINGS@ROBBKOWALSKI.COM.

Connect with me personally on social media, follow @RobBKowalski on Instagram, Facebook, YouTube and @RBKowalski1 on Twitter. Please feel free to send me a direct message, leave a comment, or ask me a question. I do my best to answer every one, so let's connect!

Made in the USA
Middletown, DE
21 November 2022

15271592R00083